GLOBETROTTER™

Travel Guide

SAN FRANCISCO

MICK SINCLAIR

NEW HOLLAND

NEW HOLLAND

★★★ Highly recommended
★★ Recommended
★ See if you can

This edition first published in 2002
by New Holland Publishers (UK) Ltd
London • Cape Town • Sydney • Auckland
First published in 1998
10 9 8 7 6 5 4 3 2 1

website: www.newhollandpublishers.com

Garfield House, 86 Edgware Road
London W2 2EA
United Kingdom

80 McKenzie Street
Cape Town 8001
South Africa

14 Aquatic Drive
Frenchs Forest, NSW 2086
Australia

218 Lake Road
Northcote, Auckland
New Zealand

Distributed in the USA by
The Globe Pequot Press
Connecticut

ISBN 1 85974 870 8

Publishing Manager: John Loubser
Managing Editor: Thea Grobbelaar
DTP Cartographic Manager: Genené Hart
Editors: Melany McCallum, Mariëlle Renssen, Jane Maliepaard, Peter Duncan
Picture Researcher: Rowena Curtis
Design and DTP: Simon Lewis
Cartographers: Marlon Christmas, Éloïse Moss
Compiler: Elaine Fick

Reproduction by Hirt & Carter (Pty) Ltd, Cape Town
Printed and bound in Hong Kong by Sing Cheong Printing Co. Ltd.

Photographic Credits:
Berkeley Convention and Visitors Bureau, 105, 106; **The Bridgeman Art Library**, 96; **California Division of Tourism/ Robert Holmes**, 112; **Caroline Jones**, 29, 30, 35, 48 (bottom), 52, 72, 74; **Hutchison Library/ Bernard Régent**, 56, 95, 97; **Hutchison Library/ Melanie Friend**, 81 (bottom), 83; **Hutchison Library/ Pierrette Collomb**, 108; **Hutchison Library/Richard House**, 81 (top); **Hutchison Library/Robert Aberman**, 37, 57, 77; **Life File/Aubrey Slaughter**, 10, 34, 45, 49, 50, 53, 63, 68, 75, 87, 88, 89, 90, 98; **Life File/Graham Buchan**, 22 (top), 44 (top); **Life File/Guy Usher**, 26, 36; **Life File/Mike Maidment**, 17, 24, 28 (top), 94; **Life File/Sally Woodward**, 22 (bottom), 78; **Mary Evans Picture Library**, 14, 15, 16; **Neil Setchfield**, cover, 4, 11, 18, 20, 21, 23 (top and bottom), 25, 27, 33, 38 (left and centre), 39, 40, 43 (top), 44 (bottom), 47, 48 (top), 58, 64, 65, 66, 67, 80, 82, 84, 93, 109, 110; **Photobank/ Adrian Baker**, 59, 111; **PictureBank Photo Library Ltd**, 6, 7, 54, 60; **Retna Pictures Ltd/J.Acheson**, 103; **Travel Ink/Ronald Badkin**, 1, 43 (bottom); **Travel Ink/Trevor Creighton**, 8, 55; **Travel Ink/Walter Wolfe**, 19; **Val Whitchelo**, 13, 71, 76; **Zefa Picture Library (UK) Ltd**, 9, 28 (bottom), 100.

Cover: *Alamo Square, with the Financial District behind.*
Title page: *Dawn breaks over the Golden Gate Bridge.*

CONTENTS

POWELL
AND
MARKET
HYDE AND BEACH
FISHERMANS
WHARF
5
Meet me
at the
St. Francis

1 Introducing San Francisco

Set on the tip of the hilly San Francisco peninsula, bounded by the Pacific Ocean to the west, the Golden Gate to the north and San Francisco Bay to the east, San Francisco enjoys the most enviable setting imaginable. Even the regular fogs that swirl into San Francisco Bay, wrapping the **Golden Gate Bridge** and **Downtown**'s skyscrapers in a transient white blanket, serve only to heighten the natural drama that surrounds this city.

Since the mid-19th-century gold rush boosted its population from 500 to 25,000 in two years and helped make it the ninth-largest city in the USA by the turn of the 20th century, San Francisco has been a place of opportunity, and has regularly set the social and cultural pace for the rest of the USA, and often the world. Openness to new ideas and unconventional lifestyles saw the city give birth to the **Beat Generation** and the **hippies**, and enabled gay men and lesbians to be integrated into the city's political machine. From the mid-1980s, San Francisco gained pioneering multi-media companies and through the 1990s was among the global leaders of the internet revolution.

Getting to know San Francisco is easy, as many of the city's neighbourhoods and sights are within close proximity of one another and can even be explored on foot. Indeed, the entire city – some 7 miles (11km) from bay to ocean – can be crossed in 20 minutes by bus. Also within easy reach are **Bay Area** settlements such as **Berkeley**, **Oakland** and **Marin County**'s desirable hillside enclaves, all inextricably entwined with San Francisco despite being highly individualistic self-governing communities.

Top Attractions

***** San Francisco Museum of Modern Art:** stunning building, stunning collection.
***** Chinatown:** intensely atmospheric ethnic area.
***** Alcatraz Island:** former prison – engrossing tours.
***** Golden Gate Bridge:** spectacular engineering in a marvellous natural setting.
***** Haight-Ashbury:** Victorian houses, wacky shops, former hippie 'home'.
***** Golden Gate Park:** a magnificent city park holding two superb art museums.
***** Oakland Museum of California:** the Golden State's nature, art and history.

Opposite: *A cable car tops the brow of one of San Francisco's 43 hills.*

Above: *The city at night across the San Francisco-Oakland Bay Bridge.*

Fact File

Population: 801,377 (2000), the US's 14th largest city. Combined with San Francisco, the Bay Area has a population of 6 million and is the nation's fifth largest metropolitan area.
Area: 46.4 sq miles (120.2km²).
Highest point: 938 ft (286m).
City parks: the city's parks have a combined area of 8,100 acres (3278ha), the largest being the 1017-acre (411.6ha) Golden Gate Park.
National park: Golden Gate National Recreation Area, the world's largest urban park, fills some 75,000 acres (30,352ha) on both sides of the Golden Gate including 28 miles (45km) of coast.
Miles of streets: 849.9 miles (1367km).
Hills: 43

THE LAND

In contrast to Los Angeles' unchecked urban sprawl, San Francisco fills a compact area of 46.4 sq miles ($120.2km^2$), thanks to its location surrounded by water on three sides. The city holds just under 724,000 people, but over a million more – who might well consider themselves San Franciscans – live elsewhere in the **Bay Area**, which includes not only San Francisco (always referred to as **'the city'**) but East Bay communities such as Berkeley and Oakland and much of Marin County, which lies directly north of the city across the Golden Gate and includes Sausalito, Tiburon and Mill Valley among the numerous rustic though wealthy hamlets secreted in the folds of its hills.

To the south, the city dissipates into a mixture of featureless suburbia and shoulder-to-shoulder industrial parks that line San Francisco Bay – a sight that greets arrivals as they head towards the city from the international airport.

San Francisco's Neighbourhoods

San Francisco comprises numerous clearly defined neighbourhoods, each with its own history, architecture, population, and atmosphere. While the compact nature of the city may make such pronounced differences surprising, it means that San Francisco is both satisfying and easy to explore in depth. The city is justifiably famous for its **43 hills**, a fact that its grid-style street layout takes no account of whatsoever. A few streets actually become staircases in their steepest sections and local drivers take special care of their clutches. Yet while an exhausting climb may be required simply to reach the next corner, San Francisco compensates for the physical effort with photogenic outlooks by the score – few cities enjoy such a proliferation of views.

Aside from such natural high points, some of the best views across and beyond the city are from the office towers that dominate **Downtown San Francisco**, the main commercial area and focal point of the city's excellent public transport routes. Nearby, **Chinatown** is among San Francisco's most celebrated ethnic areas, as is neighbouring **North Beach**, settled by Italians from the 1890s and overflowing with dozens of atmospheric cafés and perhaps San Francisco's best concentration of restaurants. On the **Northern Waterfront**, the tourist-aimed Fisherman's Wharf marks the departure point for ferries to the former prison on Alcatraz Island. Those who visit San Francisco with money to burn stay in the luxury hotels congregated on **Nob Hill**, an affluent summit since the late 19th century. If they decide to stay, they buy a generously proportioned house in **Pacific Heights**, a domicile of the rich and famous enhanced by attractive parks, architecturally intriguing homes and a chic shopping strip.

The City is Not Frisco

When San Francisco was California's only city it was, logically enough, always referred to simply as 'the city'. The habit continues today across northern California as well as in the Bay Area. It is no sin to refer to San Francisco by its full name, however, although it is not the done thing to abbreviate it to 'Frisco', a term likely to be greeted with a pained look from a local.

Below: *Lombard Street's steep drop, with Telegraph Hill in the distance.*

Above: *Fog regularly rolls in off the Pacific under the Golden Gate Bridge.*

The less materialistically motivated might find a spiritual home in **Haight-Ashbury**, the centre of hippiedom in the 1960s, a period still evoked by landmarks of psychedelia and the area's continuing anarchic leanings. Haight-Ashbury may have been created to provide a retreat from the city but these days the place to escape to is **Golden Gate Park**, with acre after acre of bucolic prettiness and the M H De Young and the California Academy of Sciences museums – two of the city's most highly regarded collections. From the mid-1980s, the disused industrial buildings of **SoMa** ('South of Market Street') were steadily transformed into the Yerba Buena Gardens complex which includes the magnificent **Museum of Modern Art** among numerous other cultural institutions. A more recent change has been the influx of high-income computer professionals to the previously low-cost apartments and houses of the still predominately Latino **Mission District**.

San Francisco Fog

The fogs that are a feature of summer mornings form over the Pacific Ocean and roll eastward, passing through the Golden Gate before burning away by noon. Certain parts of the city are particularly susceptible to fogs. On a foggy morning, find a tall building with an observation level to see the city's highest towers protruding surreally above a carpet of white. San Francisco fogs bring sounds as well as views: fog horns arranged around the coast have special tones to warn mariners of the movement of fog banks.

Climate

A temperate marine climate means San Francisco is generally mild year-round, the thermometer rarely rising above 70°F (21°C) and seldom falling below 40°F (5°C). Heavy morning fogs are common, particularly in July and August, but usually burn off quickly to reveal a bright sunny day. Fogs may return in the afternoon or evening, bringing with them a sharp drop in temperature. During September and October, when fogs are rare, San Francisco enjoys the most daily sunshine. During the winter months – November to March – the city experiences heavy rain showers; January is the wettest month, July the driest.

SAN FRANCISCO	J	F	M	A	M	J	J	A	S	O	N	D
AVERAGE TEMP. °C	9	10	11	13	14	16	16	17	17	15	12	10
AVERAGE TEMP. °F	48	50	52	55	57	61	61	63	63	59	54	50
Days of rainfall	11	11	10	6	4	2	0	0	2	4	7	10
RAINFALL mm	127	76	76	51	25	12	0	0	12	25	76	102
RAINFALL in	5	3	3	2	1	0.4	0	0	0.4	1	3	4

Earthquakes

It is no secret that San Francisco is prone to earthquakes. The city sits on the geologically unstable meeting point of the Pacific and North American plates, part of the earthquake-prone 'Ring of Fire' girdling the Pacific. Many geological fault lines lie beneath the Bay Area, including the **San Andreas** which, on average, experiences a quake large enough to be felt every three days somewhere along its 600-mile (975km) course. The **biggest earthquakes** to hit San Francisco occurred in 1865 (with an estimated magnitude of 7 on the modern Richter scale) and in 1906 (magnitude 8.3) that brought considerable damage to the city (*see* p. 16). The most recent major quake came in October 1989 when the Loma Prieta Earthquake (magnitude 7.1) caused a section of the Bay Bridge to collapse and destroyed homes in the Marina District.

Despite California leading the world in **earthquake research**, predicting when one will strike is still virtually impossible. Increased knowledge of earthquakes and how they work, however, has enabled engineers to design new, and modify old, buildings to limit the damage likely to be sustained during a major earthquake.

Earthquakes can occur at anytime but it is statistically highly unlikely that visitors will encounter a major one during their stay. If a large earthquake should strike, remember that the most **immediate danger** comes from flying glass and sharp objects. After the initial quake, be prepared for aftershocks and be alert for the dangers of leaking gas pipes and electrical short circuits.

PLATE TECTONICS

San Francisco's earthquakes are a result of sections of the earth's crust pushing against each other, an action known as plate tectonics. Most movement is gradual but pressure can be built up and eventually released as a seismic shock wave – or earthquake. Throughout California, which sits on the meeting place of the North American and Pacific plates, 18,000 quakes above magnitude 3 on the Richter scale are estimated to have occurred since 1808.
The 8.3 magnitude earthquake which destroyed San Francisco in 1906 was one of just three in excess of magnitude 8 since 1857.

Below: *Fire crews set about repairing damage inflicted by the 1989 Loma Prieta earthquake.*

SEALS AND SEA LIONS

Seals and sea lions (a non-fur-bearing seal) are commonly spotted off the California coast. Around San Francisco, the types most likely to be seen are the **harbour seal**, usually around 5ft (1.5m) long, the **California sea lion**, typically 8-9ft (2.4-2.7m) in length, and the **Stellar**, commonly 14ft (4.3m) long and noted for its noisy bark. Their numbers severely reduced by hunting from the mid-19th century onwards, seals and sea lions are now legally protected and it is actually an offence to walk sufficiently close to one to cause it to move away.

Seas and Shores

San Francisco may have a 4-mile (6km) **Pacific Ocean** shoreline but sunbathing along it is often thwarted by fogs and sharp winds, and swimming in the cold waters is made dangerous by the strong currents. A few wet-suited surfers might be spotted braving the chilly waves but the only safe swimming beach in San Francisco is China Beach (*see* p. 98) on the Golden Gate.

On the other side of the peninsula the city borders the northern limit of **San Francisco Bay**, which has a surface area at low tide of 450 sq miles (1166km^2). The bay reaches a maximum depth of 216ft (66m), but for the most part is shallow and ringed by ecologically important wetlands. Yachting and other recreational pursuits that take place on the bay disguise the fact that it is the subject of one of the most hotly contested environmental issues in California.

The major rivers of northern California meet in San Francisco Bay as they carry the snowmelt waters of the inland mountains to the ocean. The bay's brackish wetlands hold a rich assortment of insect life and microscopic organisms that provide an important source of sustenance for migratory wildfowl and, after being carried by currents into the Pacific Ocean, also feed migrating California gray whales. The diverting of the rivers to irrigate central California's farmlands and to quench the thirst of expanding southern California (which has no natural fresh water supply) has increased the saline content of the bay and threatened the wetlands. The long-term environmental impact of such measures can only be guessed at.

Below: *Rocky Ocean Beach is accessible by the coastal trail, but not safe for swimming.*

Above: *At least 600 sea lions currently reside beside Pier 39, Fisherman's Wharf.*

Wildlife

The misleadingly named **Seal Rock**, close to the Cliff House (*see* p. 99), is home to a noisy colony of **sea lions**. Found all along the California coast, these creatures with their distinctively loud bark can also be seen and heard at Fisherman's Wharf's **Pier 39**.

Serious seal-watchers visiting during December and January should make their way to **Año Nuevo State Reserve** – 42 miles (68km) south of the city – to witness the elaborate mating ritual of the bulky **elephant seal**. Weighing anything up to 4 tons, this massive seal inhabits the northern California coast.

On their annual migration from the Arctic to warmer waters off Baja California between December and March, **California gray whales** can often be spotted from the coast. Some of the best vantage points are north of the city in Marin County. Whale-watching boat trips are common and are widely advertised.

From the walking and hiking routes that weave through rugged areas such as **the Presidio** (*see* p. 93) and along the **coastal trail** (*see* p. 97), sharp observation and luck might bring sightings of **deer**, **bald eagles** (native to California), **bobcats**, and **grey foxes**. Bats and owls are among the city's nocturnally active denizens.

California's Gray Whales

Once known as devilfish for their habit of attacking whaling vessels, California (also called Pacific) **gray whales** are believed to be around 15,000 in number, declining from an estimated 25,000 in the mid-19th century, when hunting of them began in earnest. Weighing up to 40 tons, the gray whale is unique in feeding directly from the ocean floor, its tongue leaving identifiable indentations in the sea bed. With pregnant females at the head, the migration lasts several months; males and non-pregnant females often enact courtship rituals along the route.

Historical Calendar

1542 First European navigation of California coast.
1769 First sighting of San Francisco Bay, by Spanish overland expedition.
1776 The mission, San Francisco de Asís (now Mission Dolores), founded. Spanish *presidio* (or garrison) founded in the area of San Francisco still bearing that name.
1798 First California census records 833 people living in San Francisco's mission and *presidio*.
1822 California officially becomes part of Mexico.
1846 The *USS Portsmouth* berths in San Francisco (then Yerba Buena), claiming the settlement for the USA.
1847 California formally becomes a US possession.
1848 First discovery of gold in a river east of Sacramento.
1849 The peak year of the Gold Rush increases San Francisco's population by an estimated 1000%.
1856 Two men hanged by order of the Vigilante Committee, formed to combat lawlessness.
1869 The transcontinental railroad links California to the eastern USA.
1873 First cable car tested along Clay Street.
1906 The city destroyed by earthquake and fire, leaving 250,000 people homeless.
1915 Panama Pacific Exposition.
1934 Police shoot two striking dockers.
1937 Golden Gate Bridge completed.
1945 United Nations Charter signed at the Opera House.
1957 Publication of Allen Ginsberg's *Howl* launches the Beats and brings notoriety to North Beach.
1967 Thousands of hippies congregate in Haight-Ashbury in the 'Summer of Love'.
1978 Gay politician Harvey Milk and mayor George Moscone both assassinated.
1989 Loma Prieta Earthquake closes the Bay Bridge for a month.
1991 Fires spreading through the Oakland Hills destroy 3000 homes.
1995 City flags are lowered to half-mast to mourn the death of Jerry Garcia, founder member of the Grateful Dead.
1998 Multi-media companies in SoMa generate estimated annual revenue of $2 billion.
2001 SoMa is severly affected by a downturn in the e-commerce economy, leaving many San Francisco computer industry professionals jobless.

The First Ship

The first ship known to sail into what would later be called San Francisco Bay entered in 1775 under the command of **Juan Manuel de Ayala**, a Spanish navigator. Charged with exploring and mapping the area with a view to future settlement, de Ayala sailed from the Spanish base at Monterey, 120 miles (193km) south of the bay. The navigation of the bay lasted from August to September and gave many of the natural landmarks their enduring Spanish names.

HISTORY IN BRIEF

Native Habitation

Long before Europeans set foot on Californian shores there was little to encourage Native Americans – a people whose ancestors are thought to have crossed from Siberia some 6000-12,000 years ago before spreading south across what is now the USA – to settle the windswept peninsula tip that was to become San Francisco. Small communities, however, were established immediately to the north (the **Miwok**) and south (the **Ohlone**) of present-day San Francisco, supporting themselves mainly by hunting and fishing. By the time European explorers made their first known sighting of the region in the 18th century, the respective numbers of these two native American tribes totalled approximately 3000 and 10,000.

European Sightings and Landings

Although European colonial powers were established in the Americas – most notably the Spanish in South and Central America and the British on the east coast of North America – California remained a remote and uncharted region. In 1542, a Spanish ship piloted by **Juan Rodríguez Cabrillo** navigated the California coast but the first known European landing was only made 37 years later in 1579 by the British seafarer **Francis Drake**, who failed to spot the entrance to the Golden Gate and docked at a now much-disputed spot near Point Reyes, north of San Francisco.

The first sighting of San Francisco Bay, a magnificent natural harbour, invisible from the ocean, was eventually made in 1769 by a Spanish overland expedition led by **Gaspar de Portolá**. By this time the Spanish had begun establishing their chain of missions right across California – the first European settlements in the region.

Native Demise and Revival

Some 300,000 native peoples were thought to live in California at the time of European arrival but by 1913 only 17,000 remained. Spanish settlement not only brought Catholicism, which eroded native cultures, but **diseases** such as chicken pox and measles to which the indigenous population had no immunity. After the Gold Rush, further decimation resulted from white settlers' demands for land. Not until the 1960s was there government acknowledgement and financial compensation for the purloining of native peoples' land. The number of Californians now claiming Native American ancestry is around 250,000.

European Settlements

While the Spanish missions had an obvious religious purpose – the conversion of Native Americans to Catholicism – they also served to cement Spain's grip on California when rival colonial powers were looking to expand their influence in North America. The missions made use of native labour to become self-sufficient, many turning large acreages of rough scrub into farmland.

The mission of **San Francisco de Asís** (now called **Mission Dolores**), founded in 1776, gave its name to the bay (and later the city) but failed to flourish, partly through its remoteness and also as a result of Spain's decline as a colonial force.

Below: *The early Spanish chapel, Mission Dolores, dates back to 1776.*

SAM BRANNAN

Just one of many extraordinary figures to feature in the city's formative years, **Sam Brannan** landed in San Francisco in 1846 as part of a shipload of Mormons arriving from the US's east coast to begin a new life. Besides being convicted of embezzling Mormon funds, Brannan gave San Francisco its first newspaper, the **California Star**, and its first flour mill. Amassing a fortune, Brannan founded the northern California spa town of Calistoga but reputedly managed to drink his way through his funds and died in 1889 as a penniless alcoholic.

The Californios and Yerba Buena

In 1821, Mexico's independence from Spain brought it control of California. The **Californios** (people of Spanish or Mexican descent born in California) effectively took control of the region and usurped the farmlands of the former missions.

Near the site of today's Financial District, a settlement called **Yerba Buena** (meaning 'good herb', derived from the fragrant herb that grew in abundance in the area) took root as a trading outpost. The few hundred inhabitants of the outpost were mainly involved in the export of hides and tallow and the import of finished goods.

US Annexation

The westward expansion of the USA and the escalating influence of the country in the affairs of the *Californios* made California a prime target for US annexation. Through the summer of 1846, meeting little opposition, US forces made landings in all the main California settlements, including Yerba Buena (soon renamed San Francisco) on 9 July.

Below: *Farm worker J W Marshall finds the first flakes of gold in the American River; Marshall himself never benefited from the find and later died penniless.*

Discovery of Gold

In January 1848, a farm worker discovered flakes of gold in a river east of Sacramento, a then modestly sized settlement 85 miles (137km) inland from San Francisco. Washed down over millions of years from the foothills of the Sierra Nevada Mountains, California gold was, to all intents and purposes, there for the taking. With communications within California and across the USA being unreliable, the news was slow to spread and many simply did not believe it.

In San Francisco, a larger-than-life newspaper owner and businessman, **Sam Brannan**, heard of the discovery but suppressed the news until he had filled his own hardware shop with gold-prospecting tools.

The 49ers

As the truth of the discovery was accepted, California was on the receiving end of one of the biggest movements of people the world had ever seen. Throughout 1849, the Gold Rush brought tens of thousands of gold seekers – nicknamed the 49ers – from the USA and elsewhere, mostly single men. While some travelled overland from the eastern US, the majority arrived by boat. In two years, San Francisco's population swelled from 800 to 25,000. Many of the arrivals stayed in San Francisco only long enough to equip themselves for an attempt at instant riches in the nearby gold-bearing areas. San Francisco became a vast shanty town where the only pastimes were drinking and gambling (prostitution would have provided a third vice, were it not for the scarcity of women). Astute entrepreneurs, who provided services at greatly inflated prices – sometimes 10 times higher than in the eastern US – became the real beneficiaries of the Gold Rush.

Above: *49ers turn their attention from California's rivers to the richer gold-bearing seams in the ground.*

The Gold Rush

Very soon, the rivers had yielded all their gold and attention turned to the gold-bearing seams beneath the ground. These could only be reached by mining and many one-time prospectors became paid employees of new mining companies, financed by newly wealthy entrepreneurs who also invested heavily (and very successfully) in plots of San Francisco land.

Although the mine labourers endured horrific working conditions, the mines and their owners reaped enormous profits. In the peak year of 1852, the value of gold mined in California was in excess of $81 million.

While most miners lived inland in towns jerry-built around their workplace, San Francisco quickly became one of the USA's main ports and acquired a population that placed it among the country's 10 largest settlements. However, San Francisco's sudden growth prevented the creation of a proper city infrastructure.

Through the 1850s, the mostly wood-built city was frequently ravaged by fires. These were often started by

The Big Four

The most spectacular Gold Rush riches were made by four Sacramento storekeepers: Charles Crocker, Mark Hopkins, Collis P Huntington and Leland Stanford, collectively known as the Big Four. Through their subsequent ownership of the Central Pacific Railroad Company, the four dishonestly acquired federal grants for building the western section of the transcontinental railroad and acquired unprecedented political power. Deeply unpopular for their arrogance and monopolistic practices, the Big Four each lavished millions of dollars on the first Nob Hill mansions, only to see them destroyed by the 1906 earthquake and fire.

Above: *Sacramento Street around 1880, the buildings nearly all of wood.*

criminal gangs intent on looting. The inadequacies of the minuscule police force encouraged vigilante committees formed by merchants eager to protect their wealth, and several public hangings resulted.

The Barbary Coast

The scarcity of women in San Francisco during the Gold Rush was soon rectified. Besides an influx of well-bred society ladies and those who arrived to fill the labour shortage in legitimate occupations, were the many women of the so-called Barbary Coast, a waterside area (including Jackson Square and much of today's Financial District) notorious for its prostitution. The earthquake and fire razed much of the area and California's first anti-prostitution laws soon followed. Among the Barbary Coast's sleaziest sections was the two-block Morton Street, now the chic Maiden Lane (*see* p. 39).

Depression and Disaster

From the 1860s, the completion of the transcontinental railroad, linking California with the eastern USA, and the rash of mansions built on the exclusive Nob Hill, seemed to confirm the financial indestructibility of San Francisco and its moneyed elite. The collapse of Nevada's silver mines shattered the city's banks, however, and helped to plunge it into a period of economic depression. The very rich had the funds to survive but even they had no resistance to earthquakes.

Earthquake and Fire

At 05:12 on 18 April 1906, San Franciscans were awakened by an earthquake measuring 8.3 on the Richter scale. As gas mains ruptured, fires broke out across the city. A quake-damaged water supply meant the fires could not be contained and they soon combined forces, sweeping from the Financial District west across the city.

As martial law was declared, suspected looters were shot and thousands gathered for shelter in Golden Gate Park. After three days, a fortuitous change in the weather helped the fire burn itself out but not before inflicting colossal damage.

The fire left 250,000 homeless and destroyed 28,000 buildings across an area of almost 3000 acres (1214ha). Estimates of the number killed range from 700 to 3000.

Recovery and Regeneration

The devastated city made a miraculous recovery. By 1909, 20,000 new buildings had arisen from the rubble, among them the Civic Center complex crowned by the new City Hall. Though officially marking the opening of the Panama Canal, the 1915 **Panama Pacific Exposition** was acknowledged as San Francisco's signal to the world that it had recovered. Staged across a 600-acre (243ha) site around what is now the Marina District, the 10-month-long expo was attended by 20 million people. California's expanding agriculture and industry helped San Francisco prosper through the 1920s though the national depression of the 1930s was marked by bitter labour disputes, which at one point found the city crippled by a **general strike** following the fatal shooting of two dock workers by police. Through the late 1930s, the building of the **Golden Gate** and **Bay bridges** provided employment and greatly improved communications across the Bay Area. The entry of the USA into **World War II** in 1940 brought San Francisco a massive ship-building industry and an expanding population to provide labour, including the first major arrival of African-Americans from the racially divided states of the US's southeast.

The Golden Gate International Exposition

Fond memories of the 1915 Panama Pacific Exposition and a mood of civic elation following the completion of the Golden Gate and Bay bridges, encouraged the decision to stage another exposition in 1939. **Treasure Island** was created in the bay as the venue for what was titled the Golden Gate International Exposition. Opening in February 1939, the exposition attracted 10 million people but its theme of international harmony was not helped by the outbreak of World War II. In 1940 the loss-making exposition closed and Treasure Island became a naval base.

Below: *Joseph Strauss oversaw the construction of the Golden Gate Bridge.*

Above: *Writer Jack Kerouac was a leading voice of the Beat Generation.*

Immediately after the war, the creation of the **United Nations** was formally agreed upon by representatives who met at San Francisco's Opera House; only a veto by the Soviet Union prevented the city becoming the UN's permanent home.

The 1950s and 1960s

In 1957, the storm of publicity surrounding the publication of Allen Ginsberg's poem, *Howl*, by the North Beach-based City Lights bookstore, brought national attention to the writers and artists living in North Beach's low-rent apartments and meeting in its cafés – the so-called **Beat Generation**. Although the movement originated in New York in the 1940s, the Beats – misfits in the materialistic post-war USA – found a spiritual home in San Francisco, tolerant of the unconventional since Gold Rush times.

By the mid-1960s, the Bay Area was experiencing the birth of **student protest** on the university campus at Berkeley. Marches and sit-ins, which were at first limited to campus issues, soon grew into opposition to US involvement in Vietnam. In Haight-Ashbury, the much more anarchic **hippie movement** was evolving. The comparative handful of neighbourhood idealists, who envisioned a future built on music and hallucinogenic drugs, were swamped by a mass influx of disaffected youth during the summer of 1967.

Advocating armed self-determination for black Americans, the **Black Panthers** were founded in Oakland in 1966. Highly influential as well as confrontational, the group provided a focal point as violent racial unrest spread through the US's major cities, though lost influence as key members were imprisoned.

The changing sexual mores of the 1960s led to grow-

Ronald Reagan's 1960s

The turbulent 1960s coincided with the state governorship of future US president Ronald Reagan. Elected in 1966, Reagan's time as California's chief executive was marked by spending cuts in higher education, welfare and medical care, and by a readiness to use force against protest. In 1969, Reagan called on the National Guard to aid Berkeley police in regaining what had been dubbed (and what is still called) **Peoples Park**, a patch of university-owned land adopted by students and radicals. Amid the ensuing teargas and buck shot, one person died and another was blinded. The National Guard occupied the Berkeley campus for 17 days.

ing numbers of **gay** and **lesbian** San Franciscans being open about their sexual orientation. Same-sex love was nothing new in San Francisco, but such openness about it was and led to the gay and lesbian community becoming active in city politics from the 1970s.

1970s to the Present

Through the 1970s, the **Castro** district became increasingly settled by gays and lesbians whose sheer numbers gave them a potentially powerful voice in city affairs. In 1977, **Harvey Milk** became the country's first openly gay city official.

While many in San Francisco were supportive of the gay agenda, among those who were not was Dan White, a policeman turned city **politician** who assassinated Milk and mayor George Moscone, in 1978. Widespread disapproval of the token sentence passed on White resulted in 50,000 people marching on City Hall.

Although nothing to compare with 1906, San Francisco and the Bay Area continues to receive its share of **natural disasters**. The **Loma Prieta Earthquake** of 1989 was centred many miles south but caused considerable damage to the Marina District and raised doubts about the safety of the Bay Bridge. Two years later, fires raged for several days across the **Oakland Hills**, razing 3000 homes and dropping ash on San Francisco's streets.

Nature aside, perhaps the most pressing concern of the 1990s has been the city's **homeless population**. Estimates suggest that up to 10,000 people are living on San Francisco's streets at any one time. Despite much heated debate in City Hall, a workable solution seems as far away as ever.

LOS ANGELES REARS UP

At the dawn of the 20th century, San Francisco had no rivals as the major city of California. The 1906 earthquake and fire, however, helped set the scene for a shift in power within California from north to south, epitomized by the growth of Los Angeles. With no fresh water supply and no natural harbour, Los Angeles gained a railway only through bribery and, as it expanded, began drawing its fresh water from northern California's rivers. The ecological impact of this action is still being felt and underpins much of the ongoing political tensions between the **north** and the **south** of the state.

Below: *The influence of the 1960s hippie movement in San Francisco lives on.*

SILICON VALLEY

The birthplace of the personal computer was Silicon Valley, a nickname for the computer-industry dominated Santa Clara Valley that lies 55 miles (90km) south of San Francisco around the city of San Jose. Through the 1980s, the rise of the PC brought thousands of new jobs and new companies to the area, and saw property values rising by 3% per month. The spectacular financial ups and downs of the locally based Apple Computer Company epitomizes the industry's sharp-changing fortunes, however. Save for a few multimillionaire software company overlords, few in Silicon Valley consider their jobs secure.

GOVERNMENT AND ECONOMY

Elected by popular mandate for a four-year term, the **mayor** of San Francisco is the chief executive both of the city and of the county of the same name. The mayor appoints numerous officials and committee members and is responsible for most city departments. Working with his or her advisors, the mayor prepares an annual budget for the approval of the **Board of Supervisors**. Like the mayor, the 11-member Board of Supervisors is elected by popular ballot and serves as balance to the power enjoyed by the mayor.

San Francisco is a major gateway of **trade and finance** between the USA and the countries of the Pacific Rim. Through the 1980s, the booming Asian 'tiger economies' served to strengthen the city's importance as a financial centre. The **port of San Francisco** is one of the largest in the country. The Bay Area is a major manufacturing centre with most finished goods being light industrial products such as textiles and electrical appliances; pharmaceuticals are another important local product. Proximity to Silicon Valley and the rise of the internet helped the Bay Area become a significant centre of e-commerce in the 1990s.

The major player in the city's economy, however, is **tourism**. San Francisco is the most visited city in the USA and each year hosts around 13 million people. Arriving as tourists, business travellers and convention delegates, these visitors inject some $2000 million into the economy annually.

Below: *San Franciscans relax at lunchtime in Downtown's Union Square.*

THE PEOPLE

Ethnic and Religious Mix

Since the Gold Rush brought arrivals from all over the world, San Francisco has been a place where diverse ethnic and religious communities have lived side by side. The multicultural influx continues into the present, steadily eroding the size – and ultimately the power and influence – of the city's Anglo-American and European-descent population. Nowadays every third San Franciscan comes from a home where a language other than English is spoken.

Europeans

Anglo-Americans and people of European descent predominate in San Francisco, but they are derived from many countries and worship many faiths. In the 1940s, the strongly **Italian** North Beach community supported five Italian-language newspapers and had a population of some 60,000 Italian-Americans. San Francisco can still claim the USA's largest population of Italian descendants but while North Beach retains its Italian churches, community centres and restaurants, Italian-Americans – thought to number approximately 100,000 – are now spread throughout the city.

Nineteenth-century **Irish** immigration did much to influence San Francisco's growth. At times, the Irish dominated the police force, the construction trades, and the city's political machine. As they tended to frequently move from one area to another, there are few obvious vestiges of the Irish presence remaining, although the Irish tricolour that decorates the interior of St Patrick's Church in SoMa is one and the huge St Patrick's Day Parade, joined by many of San Francisco's estimated 50,000 Irish-Americans, is another.

Though smaller than the Irish, San Francisco's 25,000-strong **Russian** community is more easily traced; in the **Richmond District** there are numerous Russian-owned businesses including cafés and bakeries dispensing Russian specialities, as well as the imposing Holy Virgin Cathedral, a seat of the Orthodox religion.

LATIN AMERICANS

Among the 50,000 Latin Americans living in and around the Mission District are many Nicaraguans, Hondurans and Salvadoreans who fled the social and political turmoil of Central America during the 1970s and 1980s. In the Mission District they became part of a Spanish-speaking community established through the 1940s when the need for labour in wartime industries coupled with the district's affordable housing caused some 8000 Latin Americans to settle here. Not least because of the community's comparatively high birth rate, San Francisco's Latin American population is expected to grow significantly over the next few decades.

Below: *San Francisco is on the whole a safe city, with the San Francisco Police Department maintaining a high profile.*

Above: *Bilingual street sign in Chinatown.*
Below: *Entertaining the crowds at the popular Fishermans's Wharf .*

Asians

Racial hostility encouraged the confinement of the 26,000-strong **Chinese** community in **Chinatown** during the 1890s, while distance from mainstream Western society was furthered by the dictates of the Manchu dynasty. The destruction wrought by the earthquake and fire of 1906, and the political upheavals in China a few years later, saw a new Chinatown emerge and the Chinese become more integrated into city life. An estimated 150,000 of today's San Franciscans have Chinese ancestry, and while the community has spread far beyond Chinatown, many return there to shop and to visit the temples.

Japanese were established in San Francisco by the 1920s but with the entry of the USA into World War II in 1941 many lost their homes and businesses as the country's entire Japanese-American community was interned. Around 12,000 Japanese now live in the Bay Area, and there is a concentration of Japanese shops and businesses, and Shinto and Buddhist temples, in **Japantown**.

Aside from a widely scattered **Thai** population, arrivals from Southeast Asia have generally been a more recent feature. **Cambodians** and **Vietnamese**, the majority arriving as refugees, have become a feature of the low-rent Tenderloin neighbourhood, many opening hole-in-the-wall restaurants.

African Americans

The prospect of work in wartime industries, and the lack of opportunities in the racially segregated southeastern states, caused many African Americans to travel across the country and settle in San Francisco during the early 1940s. Many found homes in the Western Addition (an area involuntarily vacated by interned Japanese-Americans) and in purpose-built accommodation at Hunters Point, southeast of the city close to the shipyards. San Francisco's African-American population now numbers around 85,000.

Filipinos and Koreans

The Sunday mass at St Patrick's Church conducted in Tagalog, the predominant dialect of the Philippines, reflects the fact that some 33,000 Filipinos live in San Francisco. Living throughout the city and working in many trades and professions, Filipinos are rarely visible as a sizeable ethnic group. Much the same applies to the smaller numbers of Koreans in the city. During the 1950s, some Korean women came as brides of Americans following the Korean War, though many more arrived following the easing of immigration restrictions in the 1970s.

Left: *Local cyclists take a breather in Sausalito, with the city behind them.*
Below: *Traffic signs direct drivers to San Francisco's long established Chinese and Italian neighbourhoods.*

The City's Gay and Lesbian Population

San Francisco has had a history of tolerance since the Gold Rush, when some of the city's almost exclusively young, male population – distanced for the first time from the influence of church, family and peers – experimented with same-sex love. At the end of World War II, the city was the main disembarkation point for troops returning from the Pacific. Many gays, faced with a future of **ostracization** in their hometown communities due to being dishonourably discharged, simply stayed on in San Francisco. Despite its size, the city's gay population remained underground until the 1960s when many men were able to openly express their sexual identity and settlement in the Castro (*see* p. 77) began. Today, gays and lesbians use their powerful political voice to encourage, among other things, a meaningful response to the Aids crisis.

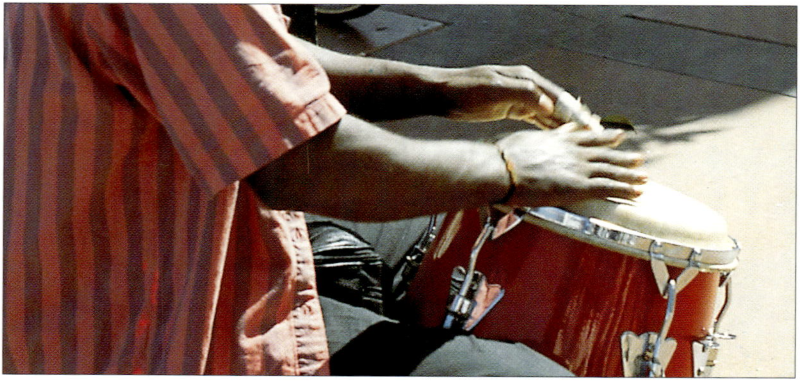

Above: *At festival time, San Francisco's streets pulsate with sound.*
Opposite: *A North Beach mural testifies to the city's rich musical heritage.*

ART

Several influential modern painters are closely linked with San Francisco and the Bay Area, including **David Park** and **Richard Diebenkorn**, both of whom worked in abstract style until adopting a figurative approach, and **Wayne Thiebaud**, noted for his depictions of San Francisco hills and streets using bold colours and distorted perspective. Among San Francisco's public art are the excellent **murals** of Coit Tower (*see* p. 49) and the **Rincon Center** (*see* p. 32), and the numerous sculptures of **Beniamino Bufano**, such as the stainless steel San Yat Sen in St Mary's Square.

Arts and Architecture

Emerging from the wild days of the Gold Rush, San Francisco quickly became the cultural hub of the US's west coast, creating much that is unique in the fields of arts and architecture.

Literature

From Mark Twain in the 1860s to the Beats of the 1950s and beyond, San Francisco's literary output has been immense and influential, though only a comparative handful of titles truly capture the city and its people.

When Dashiell Hammett's *The Maltese Falcon* appeared in 1930 it was the best evocation of San Francisco of the time; the film version of 1941 offered a brilliantly moody impression of a fog-shrouded San Francisco. More recently, Armistead Maupin's *Tales from the City* novels, evolved from newspaper vignettes, painted a humorous and insightful picture of San Francisco in the 1970s. In novel-length verse, Vikram Seth's *The Golden Gate* creatively charted the lives and loves of a handful of San Franciscans during the 1980s. Published in 1990, Amy Tan's *The Joy Luck Club* portrayed several generations of Chinese-American women. More provocatively, Jess Mowry's *Way Past Cool* offered an unsettling glimpse into black teenage life in Oakland in the nineties.

Music

Tony Bennett's *I Left My Heart In San Francisco* may be the official ballad of the city, but San Francisco is better remembered for the highly innovative rock music that percolated through Haight-Ashbury in the mid-1960s and quickly became the soundtrack for the psychedelic era. Local bands, including the Grateful Dead and Jefferson Airplane, were soon joined in popularity by Janis Joplin and, from across the bay, Country Joe and the Fish. Their concerts, enlivened by light shows and mind-expanding drugs, became the stuff of legend.

Architecture

Architects who came west but failed to make a fortune from the mid-1800s Gold Rush did at least find a city waiting to be built. Some 14,000 **Victorian** homes remain in San Francisco, many of them in impressive condition and all falling broadly into one of three styles. The earliest were the **Italianate** dwellings – several impressive specimens survive in Haight-Ashbury – intended for the rich of the 1860s. During subsequent decades advances in carpentry gave birth to the **Stick style**, with great emphasis on vertical lines, and the highly decorative **Queen Anne** look, the Haas-Lilienthal House (*see* p. 65) being one of the best examples. Influenced by the British Arts and Crafts movement, Arthur Page Brown and Willis Polk made use of shingle and other local materials in a number of acclaimed San Francisco buildings, including the 1903 **Ferry Building** (*see* p. 32). In the same period, John Bakewell and Arthur Brown raised **City Hall** (*see* 70), giving California a beaux-arts masterpiece.

More recent architecture of merit includes the 1920's **Pacific Telephone Building**, (*see* p. 73), the 1949 **Circle Gallery** (*see* p. 39), the 1972 **Transamerica Pyramid** (*see* p. 34), and the 1995 **San Francisco Museum of Modern Art** (*see* p. 74).

Film

San Francisco has been a film-makers' favourite for years, though comparatively few have captured the city well. Among those that do are *The Maltese Falcon* (1941); *Dark Passage* (1947); and *Invasion of the Bodysnatchers* (1978). The well-known high-speed car chase of the commendable *Bullitt* (1968) actually used scenes edited together from different sections of the city. Locally based film-makers include **Francis Ford Coppola**, who used Union Square for the crucial opening scenes of *The Conversation* (1974), and **Wayne Wang**, whose early low-budget movies focused on Chinatown life and developed into his critically acclaimed adaptation of Amy Tan's *The Joy Luck Club* (1993).

Above: *Though widely known as Candlestick Park, the home of San Francisco Giants and the 49ers is now officially titled 3Com Park.*

Sports and Recreation

San Francisco's professional sports teams include football's **San Francisco 49ers**, who play at 3Com Park 8 miles (13km) south of the city and baseball's **San Francisco Giants**, resident at the ultra modern Pacific Bell Park, beside the bay on Third Street. A limited number of tickets for both teams may be available from stadia box office on match days though most are sold through the agency BASS Ticketmaster; tel: (510) 762-2277. More football is found across the bay, where the **Oakland Raiders** are based at the Oakland Coliseum, as are the Bay Area's sole professional basketball team, the **Golden State Warriors**. Tickets are available through the box office and BASS ticket agency.

Those who prefer to partake in physical pursuits rather than watch them, will find San Francisco has two excellent scenic **cycling routes**: one runs between Golden Gate Park and Lake Merced in the southwest of the city; and the other explores parts of the city before crossing the Golden Gate Bridge into Marin County.

Bike rental outlets are numerous and include American Bike Rentals, tel (415) 931–0234, and Blazing Saddle Bike Rentals, tel (415) 202–8888. Many San Franciscans are keen joggers and the city caters to them with a choice of picturesque and pleasantly breezy **jogging routes**, including Golden Gate Park, Marina Green, and the Golden Gate Promenade between Fisherman's Wharf and Fort Point National Historic Monument.

Over 100 **tennis courts** can be used for free on a first come, first served basis by contacting the San Francisco Recreation and Park Department, tel: (415) 753-7001. More adventurously, the tall, windy cliffs of Fort Funston, to the south of the city, provide an excellent launching pad for hang-gliders.

Roller Skating

Roller skating competes with jogging and cycling for popularity among fitness-conscious San Franciscans, and many are adept on both conventional skates and the newer, in-line skates (the wheels arranged in line rather than at each corner, thereby increasing speed but making stopping and turning difficult at first). Rental outlets, usually offering both types of skate as well as protective wristbands and kneepads, are found in many locations, particularly along Stanyan Street in Haight-Ashbury, facing Golden Gate Park – an excellent skating location.

Food and Drink

With the city boasting some **4000** restaurants, eating in San Francisco spans everything from pretty plates of **California Cuisine** to the filling fare on offer in all-American coffee shops. Prices are seldom excessive – only the most elaborate dinner in a luxurious setting will seriously dent your budget – and standards of quality and service are usually high. **Smokers** should be warned that doing so is illegal in restaurants, cafés, bars, nightclubs and all public buildings.

Best eaten in a local diner or coffee shop, San Francisco **breakfasts** range from the US high-cholesterol standard, offering a choice of omelettes or eggs fried to order, with or without hash browns (grated fried potato), toast (wholewheat, rye, or white), ham, bacon and sausages, to freshly prepared pancakes, waffles, croissants and pastries. Some establishments offer a selection of ultra-healthy dishes built around fresh fruit and wholegrain cereals. California's omelettes commonly include three separate fillings, one of which is usually cheese – Swiss, Cheddar, American or the California-made Monterey Jack.

Dining

While some diners and coffee shops serve **breakfast** around the clock, it is usually available from 07:00. **Lunch** is generally eaten between 11:30 and 14:00. Dinner is often served from 17:30 until around 23:00. **Costs per person** excluding tip will typically be $5-8 for breakfast, for lunch $9-14. An extravagant **dinner** with wine can easily total $75-120 for two, though an average two-course evening meal is likely to cost around $35 for two, excluding drinks. A **tip** of 15-20%, depending on the quality of the service, should always be added to the bill.

Below: *A popular North Beach restaurant where all main courses feature garlic.*

Above: *Dungeness crab, in season from mid-November to June, is a speciality.*

Wine

The quality and diversity of Californian wines has helped many San Franciscans become discerning wine drinkers. The **Napa** and **Sonoma** valleys, heart of California's so-called Wine Country, lie an hour's drive north of the city and produce 90% of the wine consumed in the USA. Most bars and restaurants have a good stock of Californian wines. With little snobbery attached to wine drinking, the staff are usually ready and willing to advise on selection. The dry white Chardonnay is always dependable, though one California curiosity is **Zinfandel**, available as a white wine despite the Zinfandel grape (a type unknown outside the USA) being red.

For **lunch**, most diners and coffee shops offer an inexpensive assortment of sandwiches (entire meals between your choice of bread) and some have tasty homemade soups served by the cup (for a snack) or bowl (for a meal). In slightly smarter establishments, a California salad is a wise choice as a main dish. This typically features a deep bed of lettuce heaped with cheese, strawberries, grapes, avocado, orange slices, and much more, depending on what is in season.

Many Chinese restaurants offer excellent **dim sum** at lunchtime. These small pastries filled with meat, seafood or vegetables are wheeled through the dining room on trolleys and ordered by customers as the waiter or waitress passes.

Their atmosphere may range from the refined to the anarchic, but the city's innumerable **cafés** almost all offer a good assortment of light meals and snacks. Big eaters on tight budgets will find that **buffets** served by many restaurants at lunchtime (by fewer at dinner time), offer a chance to eat as much you can for a price roughly equivalent to that of a standard menu meal.

Afternoon tea is in vogue among San Francisco high society and served by many of the city's poshest hotels in sumptuous surrounds. Besides a choice of quality teas, participants are served bite-sized sandwiches and an array of delicate cakes and pastries.

For many San Franciscans, going out for **dinner** is a vital part of everyday life and local newspaper

restaurant reviews are avidly read. Predictably, the more you spend the better the meal and the surrounds are likely to be, though the impact of 1970's **California Cuisine** – small, perfectly prepared and artistically arranged meals based on the freshest local ingredients and the chef's blending of recipes from near and far – has filtered down into the medium-priced eateries. The best bet in many quality restaurants is the **nightly special**, which will make the most of seasonal fare and the chef's inspiration.

Certain neighbourhoods are noted for their **ethnic cuisines**: North Beach has a tremendous assortment of quality Italian eateries, and Chinatown and the Richmond District hold numerous Chinese and a sprinkling of Vietnamese and Cambodian restaurants. Thai cooking is prevalent throughout the city and is usually of an excellent standard, as are the fewer outlets offering Indian and African fare. Latin-American food is easily found in the Mission District, where Mexican, Salvadorean and Guatemalan restaurants are in evidence, alongside a few Argentinian, Peruvian and Chilean eateries.

San Francisco has its share of local **specialities**. These include the creamy **Dungeness crab**, in season from mid-November to June and served in many styles; the Italian fish dish **cioppino**, stew-like chunks of fish and shellfish in a tomato sauce; and **linguine with clams**, another local Italian seafood staple. Ideal for snacks, the chewy, slightly bitter **sourdough bread** has been a San Francisco favourite since the Gold Rush and is widely found. At Fisherman's Wharf many snackstands offer a hollowed-out sourdough crust filled with **clam chowder**, a kind of stew.

For vegetarians, San Francisco is a culinary delight. There are nearly always plenty of vegetarian options to choose from, and those restaurants which do specialise in meats are rare.

Beers, Cocktails and Spirits

California is in the throes of a **micro-brewery** revolution with a growing number of dedicated beer makers producing notable beers in small breweries usually joined to a bar or restaurant, and San Francisco has several of these. Most bars also have a range of **American beers** such as *Budweiser*, *Coors* and *Miller*, and stronger **imported brews** such as *Heineken*, *Dos Equis* and *Tecate*. Spirits can only be served in bars and fully licensed restaurants. **Cocktails** are common; any type you might order is unlikely to perplex a properly trained bartender, who is also likely to suggest a few exotic local versions.

Above: *American beer has improved in leaps and bounds in recent years: San Francisco-brewed steam beer is worth trying.*

Opposite below: *Seafood is served in a great variety of forms.*

2
Downtown San Francisco

Wherever you are in San Francisco, your gaze will inevitably be drawn to the contemporary high-rise towers of high finance that dominate the eastern section of the city and pinpoint the location of Downtown, the business hub of San Francisco. During rush hour, the streets of Downtown San Francisco's **Financial District** are swept by a tide of sharp-suited professionals heading to or from a day immersed in the multimillion dollar realms of insurance, banking and global trading. San Francisco is an important centre for worldwide money-moving, a fact which sometimes makes this area seem one of the city's least distinctive; no different from any other major financial city.

It is a mark of San Francisco's character, however, that even here the individualistic quirks of the city shine through. The totem to capitalism that is the Transamerica Pyramid has an ecologically desirable park of redwood trees at its base, traders at the Stock Exchange have a Diego Rivera mural to call their own, public art seems to lurk on every corner, and the dainty and historic Ferry Building retains the indefinable charm that has captured San Franciscan hearts for years.

San Francisco may not be an old city but it is steeped in traditional pursuits. Shopping around Downtown's perennially fashionable Union Square is one such tradition. Here big-name **department stores** rub elegant shoulders with an array of specialist and designer shops. Also situated on Union Square is the luxurious St Francis Hotel, deeply entrenched in San Francisco history.

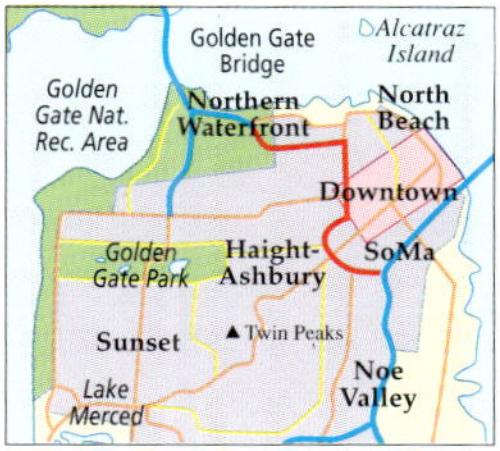

Don't Miss

*** **Ferry Building:** treasured landmark and earthquake survivor.
*** **Merchants Exchange Building:** historic seat of commerce.
** **Rincon Center:** clever modern design, brilliant 1930s murals.
** **St Francis Hotel:** steeped in San Francisco folklore.
** **Transamerica Pyramid:** an instantly recognisable feature of the city skyline.

Opposite: *The impressive Financial District, viewed from Telegraph Hill's Coit Tower.*

ARTHUR PAGE BROWN

Not be confused with (and no relation to) another San Francisco architect, Arthur Brown of City Hall fame, Arthur Page Brown worked for the revered New York architectural firm of McKim, Mead and White before heading west in 1889 and designing the Mission-style California Pavilion for an exposition in Chicago. Although best remembered for the **Ferry Building**, Brown also lent a considerable hand to another architecturally impressive structure in San Francisco, the **Swedenborgian Church** (*see* p. 66).

Opposite: *On its completion, the Ferry Building was the tallest structure in the city.*

Ferry Building **

Neighboured and dwarfed by the Financial District's chaotic cluster of high-rises, the **Ferry Building** dates from 1903. Prior to the construction of the **Bay** and **Golden Gate** bridges in the 1930s, ferries were the main form of transportation between the city and the rest of the Bay Area, and thousands of commuters passed through the Ferry Building twice daily.

Graced by a 235ft (72m) **clock tower** inspired by the Moorish belltower of Seville Cathedral in Spain, the Ferry Building was once the tallest structure in the city and was designed by the influential architect, **Arthur Page Brown**. Remaining intact through the earthquake and fire of 1906, the building became a symbol of San Francisco's survival and a much-loved local landmark.

These days, only a few ferries serve the adjacent docks and nondescript offices consume the building's interior. For a while it was obscured by the Embarcadero Freeway, built in the 1960s. However, following the 1989 earthquake, the roadway had to be demolished and the building was restored to view. The Ferry Building and the adjacent stretch of the Embarcadero are steadily becoming more visitor friendly with various outdoor events.

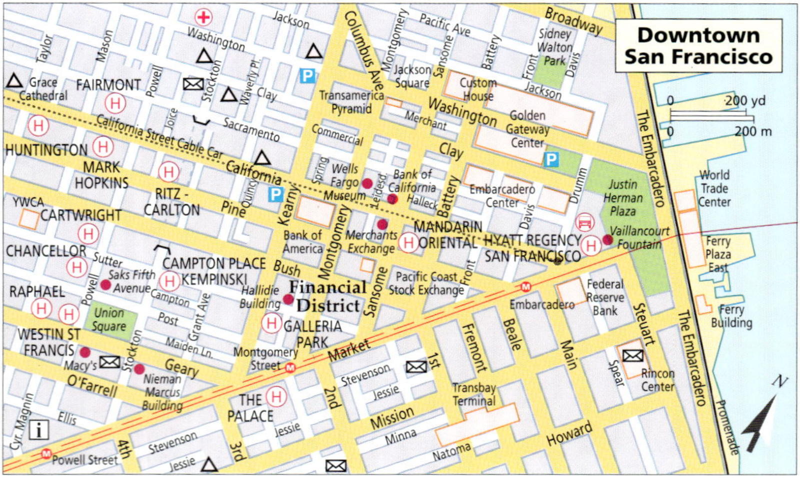

Market Street and Around

The Ferry Building stands at one end of Market Street, a thoroughfare that is 120ft (37m) wide and cuts across the city's otherwise right-angled, grid-style streets at a 36º angle – the reason for it doing so seemingly known only to the Irish engineer who laid it out in 1847. Always heavy with traffic, Market Street serves as the main artery of the Financial District and the entire city, and is where most bus routes converge.

The Unlamented Embarcadero Freeway

Among the more ill-judged pieces of San Francisco urban planning in the 1960s was the construction of the **Embarcadero Freeway**, an elevated roadway that scythed through the edge of the Financial District and blocked the Ferry Building from view. One happy by-product of the Loma Prieta Earthquake of 1989 was damage to the freeway sufficient to result in its demolition for safety reasons. This turn of events did nothing to lessen the popular belief that the Ferry Building leads a charmed life.

The Rincon Center

A block south of Market Street on the corner of Mission and Steuart streets, the **Rincon Center** is among San Francisco's more imaginative and successful adaptations of an existing building. Grafted onto the rear of an attractive 1930's post office is an expansive office, shopping and apartment complex dominated by a soaring atrium with a ceiling-to-floor fountain. Pride of place, however, goes to Anton Refregier's **murals** that line the post office walls and unsentimentally depict the violence and bloodshed of San Francisco's past. These caused great controversy on their unveiling and were condemned (and nearly destroyed) as communist propaganda in the 1950s.

Justin Herman Plaza and the Embarcadero Center *

Facing the Ferry Building to the north of Market Street is **Justin Herman Plaza**, a decidedly urban but appealing open space much enjoyed by lunching office workers, shoppers and skateboarders. What appears to be a succession of upended concrete tubes littering the plaza is actually the **Vaillancourt Fountain**, created by Canadian sculptor Arman Valliancourt in 1971. This modernistic artwork invites the public to follow the footpaths weaving under and around its cascades of water. The plaza is adjacent to the enormous **Embarcadero Center**, an eight-building multiplex of shops, restaurants and luxury hotels. On top of the Embarcadero One, the **Embarcadero Skydeck** (daily 12:00–21:00) brings spectacular over the rooftops of Financial District high-rises and far beyond across the city and Bay Area.

The Transamerica Redwood Park

While the Transamerica Pyramid is one of the best-known features of the San Francisco skyline, the ½ acre (0.2ha) **Transamerica Redwood Park** that sits at the foot of the building's eastern wall is one of the city's least-known parks. As the name suggests, the park boasts a row of redwood trees, planted in 1971 and as yet far from their maximum height. Most park users are Financial District workers enjoying a picnic lunch, though on Fridays in summer free **lunchtime classical concerts** draw larger crowds.

The Financial District

A few blocks north of the Embarcadero Center looms the unmistakable tapered profile of the **Transamerica Pyramid**. Today among the most distinctive contributions to the city skyline and widely admired, the building was loathed by many San Franciscans on its 1972 completion. The 853ft (260m) pyramid, its upper levels illuminated at night, provides a prestigious address for numerous insurance companies and other businesses. The lobby level has a collection of mildly interesting art works but more entertaining are the TV monitors of the Virtual Observation Deck linked to cameras on the building's upper reaches. Fog permitting, the screens reveal a stunning panorama of San Francisco and environs.

Across Washington Street architectural contrast is provided by a grouping of handsome brick buildings that comprise Jackson Square (not a square but simply the name of the district). Many of these effectively restored buildings date from the 1850s, survivors not only of the 1906 earthquake but also of the infamous Barbary Coast (*see* p. 16). One notable address is **732 Montgomery Street**, the former home of the *Golden Era*, an influential literary magazine established in 1852 that published the early works of Mark Twain, Bret Harte and many other soon-to-be famous writers. High-class antique shops and lawyers' and architects' offices now occupy these refreshingly human-sized structures in the shadow of modern corporate towers.

Below: *The 52-storey Bank of America Building is currently the city's highest.*

The tallest building in the city, the 52-storey **Bank of America Building** at 555 California Street, is easily spotted from Jackson Square. Completed in 1969, the building boasts a red carnelian marble façade that appears to change in colour as the sun moves across the sky, assuming golden hues at sunset and at other times appearing almost transparent. A more recent design *tour de force* is 101 California Street, a skyscraping cylinder that appears to have been mated with elements of a greenhouse. Plants are lavishly arranged around the

Above: *The unmistakable Transamerica Pyramid tapers to a point.*

atrium and benches on the plaza's concrete terrace are bedecked with greenery.

While the Financial District's modern buildings will delight anyone with an eye for contemporary architecture, perhaps more character – and equal architectural invention – is to be found amid the earlier buildings that arose as San Francisco became the economic powerhouse of the US's west coast. One fine example is the 1903 **Merchants Exchange Building**, 465 California Street. Enter through the sky-lit marble lobby, lined with model sailing ships, and directly ahead is what was originally the Grain Trading Hall, the vibrant centre of Pacific-coast wheeling and dealing. Traders here kept tabs on all Pacific shipping while a lookout on the roof yelled news of approaching vessels. The walls are lined with the epic maritime paintings of **William Coulter**, an Irishman who arrived in California in 1869 and completed these rousing depictions of San Francisco seafaring in the early 1900s. If the hall is closed, the murals can at least be glimpsed through the glass-panelled doors.

Willis Polk, one of San Francisco's most celebrated and influential architects (*see* panel), designed much of the Merchants Exchange Building and was also responsible for the contrasting 1917 **Hallidie Building**, 130 Sutter Street, claimed to be the first building in the world to hang a curtain of glass and metal in front of a concrete façade – a building technique that helped pave the way for the modern skyscraper.

Another focus of buying and selling, the **Pacific Coast Stock Exchange**, 301 Pine Street, has a neoclassical style dating from its original 1873 function as a US

Willis Polk

Linked with many of San Francisco's most acclaimed buildings, Willis Polk began making his architectural mark in the 1890s at the Chicago office of 'city beautiful' visionary Daniel Burnham, and soon headed Burnham's San Francisco office. While they share the man's imagination and ingenuity, few of Polk's San Francisco buildings share a particular style. They range from the shingle house Polk designed for himself in Russian Hill (1013–19 Vallejo Street), to the grand Merchant Exchange Building and the revolutionary Hallidie Building, to which much modern high-rise architecture owes a considerable debt.

Above: *Moving fast in San Francisco's busy Financial District.*

> **THE MAKING OF THE FINANCIAL DISTRICT**
>
> Up until the 1850s, much of what is now the Financial District was under water. The eastern shoreline of the city was originally marked by Montgomery Street from which wharves jutted into the bay. A series of fires around the foot of Telegraph Hill, the burgeoning city's first centre for financial activities, encouraged the banks located there to move the short distance south to where new streets were created by landfill. Much of the solid matter forming the new streets consisted of sunken ships, abandoned in the bay by crews eager to join the gold rush. The vessels still remain buried under today's Financial District streets.

Treasury mint. Remodelled as a stock exchange in the 1930s, the building has a pair of imposing granite sculptures on its steps that were designed by Robert Stackpole; the female group represents the fruit of the earth and the male group symbolizes mankind's ingenuity. Public admission, which is by appointment only and can be made through the Mexican Museum (tel: (415) 202 9700), is ostensibly to admire the exchange's mural painted by the Mexican master, **Diego Rivera**.

Still doing business behind the stately columns of its 1907 home, the **Bank of California**, 400 California Street, was the first financial building in what became the Financial District following the city's recovery from the earthquake and fire of 1906. Founded in 1864, the bank did much to stabilize San Francisco's economy during the city's formative years, although its failure in 1875 – due to over-investment in Nevada silver mines – plunged San Francisco into financial turmoil.

The stormy story of money and the Wild West is encapsulated by an engrossing assemblage of coins, paper money and other items in the bank's **Museum of Money of the American West** (open Monday-Thursday 10:00–16:00; Friday 10:00–17:00), which occupies a basement strong room.

Wells Fargo Museum *

Following the Gold Rush, San Francisco grew at lightning pace to become one of the US's largest cities – but also one without dependable financial institutions. A reputation for honesty and reliability, forged by its pioneering of routes across the treacherous Wild West, enabled the **Wells Fargo company** to fill this gap, eventually growing into one of the country's major banking organisations.

The Wells Fargo Museum, 420 Montgomery Street (Monday–Friday 09:00–17:00), inside a branch of the bank close to the company's original San Francisco office (opened in 1852), entertainingly documents the story of the company. An 1860's stagecoach suggests some of the deprivations of early overland travel and countless relics reveal the chaotic nature of San Francisco at the time of the gold rush.

Left: *The Wells Fargo company was instrumental in the making of San Francisco, and still has several notable branches across the city.*

Cable Cars and Clay Street

On 2 August 1873, San Francisco's **first cable car** made its initial test run along Clay Street, one of the Financial District's main arteries. This entirely novel form of transport was devised by a Scot, Andrew Hallidie. It is said Hallidie conceived the idea after seeing a horse fall and shed its load while climbing one of San Francisco's treacherous hills. Hallidie's plan called for a constantly moving steel cable beneath the street to which the passenger car would be connected by a special grip operated from inside the car. Within 30 years of the test run, San Francisco had 600 cable cars in operation.

Above: *One of Union Square's best-known department stores.*
Centre: *Resplendent in pose, the 100ft (30m) Dewey Monument.*
Opposite: *The legendary St Francis Hotel dates back to 1903.*

> **UNDER UNION SQUARE**
>
> Underground car parks are seldom the stuff of visitor interest (particularly for those without a car to park) but beneath Union Square lies one of the first examples of a beneath street-level parking space in the USA, designed by architect **Thomas Pflueger** and opened in 1942. Such was Union Square's social standing at the time, department store customers could have their vehicles valet parked and later driven to the store's entrance for collection on completion of their shopping.

Union Square

Named for its use by pro-Union elements before the Civil War, Union Square is undergoing a much needed improvement which, by its completion in late 2002, should reveal a fitting centrepiece to Downtown San Francisco. Film buffs might remember the square as it used to be by recalling the opening scenes of Francis Ford Coppola's 1974 film, *The Conversation*, which were shot here.

Above the west end of the square rises the **Dewey Monument**, a 100ft (30m) granite column topped by a figure of the Roman goddess **Victory** and intended to mark Admiral Dewey's 1898 defeat of the Spanish fleet at Manila during the Spanish-American War. San Francisco lore has it that Victory was modelled on Alma Spreckels, wife of the wealthy sugar magnate Adolph Spreckels, a member of one of the most prominent families in early San Francisco.

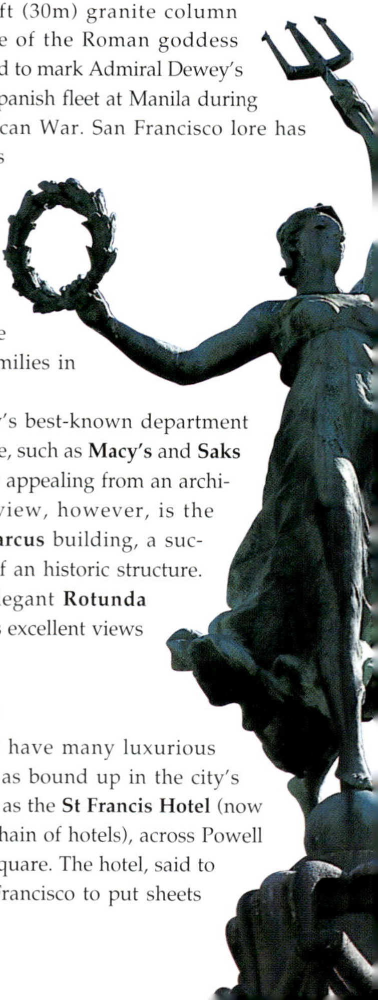

Many of the city's best-known department stores line the square, such as **Macy's** and **Saks Fifth Avenue**. More appealing from an architectural point of view, however, is the stylish **Neiman Marcus** building, a successful upgrading of an historic structure. From inside, the elegant **Rotunda Restaurant** provides excellent views across the square.

St Francis Hotel **

San Francisco may have many luxurious hotels, but few are as bound up in the city's history and folklore as the **St Francis Hotel** (now part of the Westin chain of hotels), across Powell Street from Union Square. The hotel, said to be the first in San Francisco to put sheets on its beds, opened in 1903. The grandfather clock in the expansive lobby has long been a favourite San Francisco meeting place and the adjacent **Compass Rose** lounge a popular spot among San Franciscan high society for afternoon tea and a glass or two of champagne. It was at the St Francis in the 1920s that the **Fatty Arbuckle affair** erupted, the death of a young actress being blamed by a sensation-seeking press on the then highly successful comic actor (*see* panel).

THE FATTY ARBUCKLE AFFAIR

By the 1920s, little love was lost between the Hollywood film industry and the popular press, who often sold papers by raking up film-star scandals. In 1921, screen comedian Fatty Arbuckle chose to celebrate the signing of a lucrative new contract by spending a weekend in San Francisco at the **St Francis Hotel**. The subsequent death of **Virginia Rappe** (apparently linked to her recent abortion) led to Arbuckle being accused of her murder, despite the lack of evidence against him, and being portrayed as a drunken sex-crazed beast. Arbuckle was tried and acquitted but not before the press had ruined his career.

Maiden Lane **

Perhaps the prettiest, and certainly the cleanest, non-residential street in San Francisco, **Maiden Lane** is a narrow two-block enclave in the heart of the city's busiest shopping area lined by designer stores, posh boutiques and speciality shops.

The **Circle Gallery**, 140 Maiden Lane, offers paintings and sculpture by Bay Area artists but is chiefly of note for its role as a miniature of **Frank Lloyd Wright**'s acclaimed Guggenheim Museum in New York. In the late 1940s, Wright took this 1911 building and gave it many of the features that would later grace his New York masterpiece – most obviously the spiral ramp from which the artworks can be viewed.

As you enter through the decorative wooden gates of Maiden Lane, however, ponder the fact that its current chic appearance belies a seriously sleazy past. Prior to the 1906 earthquake and fire, Maiden Lane was known as Morton Street and was among the more notorious sections of the sex-for-sale Barbary Coast.

CITY LIGHTS BOOK
CITY LIGHTS BOOKSTORE

3
Chinatown, North Beach and Telegraph Hill

Abutting the Financial District to the north, **Chinatown** is an enclave within a western city so heavily flavoured by the sights, sounds and smells of the Far East that it almost seems to be an autonomous region. The racial oppression of the Chinese almost made Chinatown separate from the rest of San Francisco in the late 1800s, and its inhabitants were rarely allowed to leave.

Today's Chinatown is an inviting place with some of the most popular restaurants in the city. Lined with everything from temples to barbers' shops, there is much to explore along busy Grant Avenue and its side streets.

A particular feature of San Francisco is that contrasting neighbourhoods are often separated by no more than the width of a street. Nowhere is this more true than between Chinatown and North Beach, where *dim sum* restaurants and herbalists give way to pizza houses and Italian delis within a few strides. In **North Beach**, where the forebears of San Francisco's many Italian-Americans first established themselves, there are scores of outstanding restaurants. The many cafés of North Beach provided meeting places during the 1950s for the Beat Generation, many of whom are still affectionately remembered – and, in some cases, are still in evidence, studiously ignoring the stares of curious patrons.

Situated above North Beach, socially and physically, **Telegraph Hill** is a well-tended hillside neighbourhood characterized by pricey homes and fabulous views. Telegraph Hill's Coit Tower is one of San Francisco's most worthwhile landmarks.

DON'T MISS

** **Bank of Canton:** traditional Chinese architecture.
*** **Chinatown:** a bustling ethnic area.
** **Chinese Historical Society of America:** documents Chinese life in California from the Gold Rush onwards.
** **Coit Tower:** decorated by powerful 1930's murals.
*** **North Beach:** a pulsating mixture of Italian cafés and Beat-era landmarks.
** **Washington Square:** North Beach's prized open space.

Opposite: *City Lights bookstore, on North Beach's Columbus Avenue.*

Grant Avenue: San Francisco's Oldest Street

Although it is hard to imagine seeing it today, Grant Avenue is officially San Francisco's oldest street, originating as little more than a muddy track named *Calle de la Fundación* ('Street of the Founding') by the Spanish-speaking population of the tiny settlement known as Yerba Buena. Under US rule, the street became **Dupont Street** before being destroyed by the 1906 earthquake and fire, and then renamed Grant Avenue in memory of President Ulysses S Grant.

CHINATOWN

Packed with restaurants, exotic shopping emporiums, groaning market stalls and beguiling herbal medicine stores, Chinatown is San Francisco's most vibrant and clearly defined ethnic area. Occupying just 24 blocks, it has an estimated population of 75,000, and forms part of the largest Asian community outside of Asia. Many Chinese, who arrived during the Gold Rush, have become wealthy enough to leave these bustling streets and alleys for more comfortable suburbs. Today's residents include many Vietnamese and Cambodians. **Grant Avenue**, Chinatown's main tourist thoroughfare, is decorated by dragon-tail entwined lamp posts, enhanced by bilingual street signs. Grant Avenue shops stock everything from souvenir chopsticks to huge, colourful kites. A block away, Chinese shoppers crowd the Stockton Street market stalls where live chickens and hard-to-identify Asian vegetables are among the fare on offer.

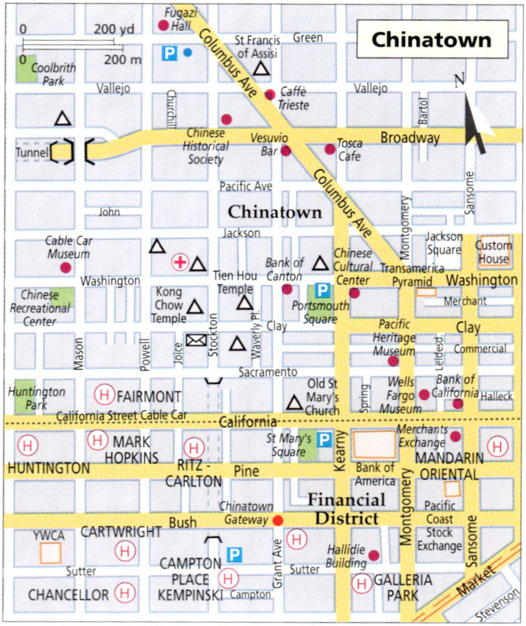

Bank of Canton **

Many Chinatown buildings have appealing Chinese architectural features. One built in full traditional style is the eye-catching **Bank of Canton**, 743 Washington Street. Sporting a bright-red, three-tier pagoda roof, the building was completed in 1909 and originally housed the Chinatown telephone exchange. The exchange's operators memorized the names and numbers of the neighbourhood's subscribers so that Chinese callers would not risk bad luck by asking for a person by number.

Side Streets, Alleys and Temples

Many visitors see no more of Chinatown than Grant Avenue but the neighbourhood lives its life away from the major thoroughfares and along a series of narrow (and by day safe) side streets and alleys. These are typically lined by newspaper vendors stocking Chinese magazines and books, barbers' shops, the odd factory making fortune cookies (an item first served in Chinatown restaurants but invented by a Japanese San Franciscan), family associations and several religious sites. One of the larger side streets, **Waverly Place**, is noted for its brightly painted balconies and is the site of what is claimed to be the community's oldest temple, **Tien Hou** (125 Waverly Place), founded in 1852. The temple's opening hours are erratic (usually daily 10:00–16:00) and you should acknowledge your good luck if you find the door unlocked by leaving a donation. Imbibe the incense-filled air and admire the wooden statue of Tien How (Goddess of Heaven and protector of, among others, travellers) behind the offerings of oranges and tangerines. Another temple meriting a visit is **Kong Chow**, 855 Stockton Street, where an evocative 19th-century shrine and statue of the deity, Kuan Di, can be viewed on the top floor of a building housing a post office.

Above: *Vibrant with commercial activity, this is typical of Chinatown's main thoroughfares.*
Left: *Chinatown Gateway stands at the foot of Grant Avenue.*

Chinatown Gateway

Straddling **Grant Avenue** at its junction with **Bush Street**, the Chinatown Gateway provides a symbolic entrance to Chinatown. It is easy to walk through it without giving it a second glance but a close look reveals dragons, carp, lions and other creatures woven into the design, their presence intended to bring luck and prosperity to the neighbourhood. While the gateway's symbolism is based on ancient Chinese traditions, the structure is a comparatively recent addition to Chinatown, unveiled in 1970.

Chinese Historical Society of America **

Located in the heart of Chinatown, the small but informative **Chinese Historical Society of America**, at 644 Broadway (open Monday–Friday 10:30–16:00), documents the arrival of the Chinese in California and the many trials and tribulations encountered by them since. Many early Chinese arrivals worked in gold mines, while others established service businesses such as laundries. Countless Chinese labourers worked on the transcontinental railroad that linked the east and west coasts of the USA in 1869. By the 1890s, however, the Chinese were being blamed for an economic decline and 'yellow peril' hysteria in the popular press led to a series of laws curbing immigration from China and limiting the rights of Chinese in the USA. The museum's exhibits include Gold Rush artefacts and religious items, and culminate in a celebration of the modern-day achievements of San Francisco-born Chinese-Americans.

> **SUN YAT-SEN IN CHINATOWN**
>
> The Manchu dynasty that ruled China until 1911 enforced strict adherence to traditional dress and customs and helped keep the Chinese of Chinatown distanced from San Francisco life. At the forefront of opposition to the emperor's rule was Sun Yat-Sen, who travelled widely in the West and stayed briefly (during 1894) in San Francisco's Chinatown before returning for a longer period (from 1904) when he published a newspaper, *Young China*, disseminating republican views.
> An impressive statue of Sun Yat-Sen stands in St Mary's Square, between California and Pine streets.

Pacific Heritage Museum *

Complementing a visit to the Chinese Historical Society of America is a look around the **Pacific Heritage Museum** (Monday–Saturday 10:00–16:00), housed in the California headquarters of the Bank of Canton, 608 Commercial Street. The museum has a two-fold role, featuring impressive changing exhibitions that focus on the arts and

history of the Pacific Rim region (with special emphasis placed on the links between China and San Francisco) and a permanent display of coins and minting devices outlining the building's original role – a branch mint for the US Treasury that started operations in 1875.

Portsmouth Square and the Chinese Cultural Center *

Nowadays very much a social centre for mostly elderly Chinese men consumed in lengthy games of dominoes, **Portsmouth Square** was the heart of Yerba Buena (as San Francisco was known) in July 1846 when a group of American sailors came ashore to declare US rule in the tiny settlement. It was here, too, in 1848 that newspaper owner **Sam Brannan** (*see* p. 14) first announced the discovery of gold in California and where a contemplative **Robert Louis Stevenson**, the Scottish writer, passed many hours awaiting his bride-to-be, Fanny Osbourne. Stevenson is remembered by a bronze plinth.

Adjacent to the square rises the architecturally uninspiring Holiday Inn, on the third floor of which is the worthwhile **Chinese Cultural Center** (Tuesday–Satuday 10:00–16:00) with changing exhibitions on Chinese arts and crafts.

Old St Mary's Church **

Incongruous as it may at first seem, the oldest Catholic cathedral on the US's Pacific Coast stands on the edge of Chinatown at 600 California Street. Completed in 1854, **Old St Mary's Church** has bricks that were shipped around Cape Horn and a granite base transported from China. The biblical quotation on the clock tower, 'Son Observe the Time and Fly from Evil', was aimed at the customers of the brothels that once filled the immediate area but were destroyed by the 1906 earthquake and fire.

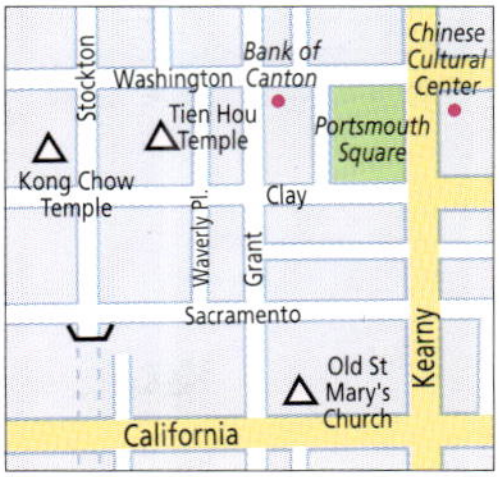

Opposite above: *Many San Franciscans regularly visit Chinatown's shops and street-side stalls.*
Opposite below: *Colour in a Chinatown restaurant.*
Left: *Old St Mary's Church once provided an English-language school for local Chinese.*

Chinatown Herbalists

Chinatown's herbalists play an important role in community life. Unlike the Western norm of visiting the doctor only when ill, the Chinese routinely consume medicinal herbs, nuts, seeds, vegetables and other items to stay healthy. The first Chinese in San Francisco spoke little English and had little faith in Western medicine (which, in any event, was usually denied them). Consequently, immigrant herbalists found a ready market among their countrymen. Inside a herbalist's shop, the stock is likely to consist of hundreds of items ranging from inexpensive ginseng root to the extremely pricey shark's fin, believed to provide energy.

North Beach Museum

For a historical insight into North Beach, go see the photographs, documents, and assorted paraphernalia at the North Beach Museum (Monday–Friday 09:00–17:00) on the mezzanine level of the Bay View Bank, 1435 Stockton Street. Many items are donated by local people, arranged into temporary exhibitions on specific aspects of North Beach life.

North Beach

The burgeoning population of Chinatown has blurred the exact geographical distinctions between it and neighbouring North Beach. But across Columbus Avenue is the unmistakable conglomeration of Italian restaurants, cafés, shops, jazz clubs, and bars that makes North Beach one of the city's busiest nightlife areas.

Its beach disappeared long ago under the landfill that pushed the city's northern waterfront to what is now Fisherman's Wharf. North Beach was settled by southern Italians in the 1890s. The community swiftly thrived, earning an enduring reputation for offering excellent food at favourable prices. By the 1950s, the neighbourhood's low rents and friendly cafés attracted many of the

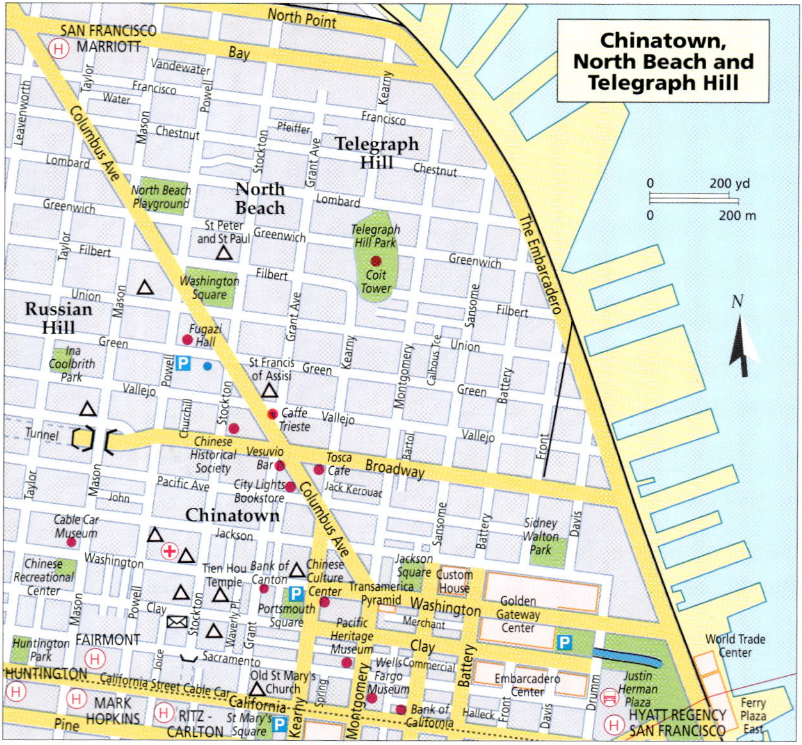

seminal figures of what became the Beat Generation – among them, Jack Kerouac, Allen Ginsberg and Lawrence Ferlinghetti. The controversy surrounding the publication of Ginsberg's poem *Howl*, in 1957, brought the Beats to national prominence and inadvertently made North Beach the centre of a mass movement of disaffected youth.

Above: *Locals engrossed in t'ai chi routines on Washington Square.*

North Beach today is a trendy and pricey area, though one that is great fun to explore as it has retained its Italian heritage and still offers plenty of landmarks to thrill fans of the Beats. The legacy of the Beats, or simply perhaps the conviviality of North Beach cafés, means that many earnest, sunglassed youths are to be seen scribbling into notebooks at tables. Alongside them, however, genuine grey-haired survivors of the Beat era might also be spotted.

Italian Landmarks

San Francisco's Italian-American population is now dispersed throughout the city, but North Beach holds many reminders of their presence. Predating the major influx of Italians, the first Catholic church founded in California since the time of the Spanish missions, the **Church of St Francis of Assisi**, partly dating from 1860, stands at 610 Vallejo Street. Much more impressive is the twin-spired **Church of Sts Peter and Paul**, on Filbert Street between Stockton and Powell streets, a Romanesque edifice that took 20 years to complete and which is gracefully illuminated by spotlights after dark.

The church stands on the north side of **Washington Square**, a small but popular green space and excellent spot for a people-watching picnic. On weekends, local artists display their works in the square. A few minutes' walk away stands the elegant terracotta façade of **Fugazi Hall**, 678 Green Street. Raised as a community centre in 1912, the hall was a gift to the people of North Beach by John Fugazi, a local banker who became one of the founders of the giant Bank of America. Besides the offices of community organizations, the hall is the venue for a long-running satirical revue, *Beach Blanket Babylon*.

Washington Square and H D Cogswell

Despite its name, Washington Square bears no marker to George (or any other) Washington but does hold a statue of **Benjamin Franklin** paid for by H D Cogswell, a prominent San Francisco dentist who arrived during the Gold Rush and used California gold to fill his patients' teeth. Now dry, taps at the base of the statue originally flowed with drinking water – what Cogswell called 'nature's own beverage'. The statue was one of a series of similar statue fountains erected by Cogswell, a fervent supporter of the temperance movement, across the country.

Topless in North Beach

Many in San Francisco associate North Beach with Italians and Beats, but a few remember the neighbourhood more fondly for the breasts of **Carol Doda**. A dancer at the **Condor Club**, 300 Columbus Avenue, Doda's breasts were exposed here in 1964 in what became the first topless dance routine in the USA. Within a few years, North Beach could also claim the first bottomless show in the country. Doda is remembered by a plaque on the wall of the **Condor Bistro**, which now occupies the site.

Right and below: *The ever-popular Vesuvio, a café and bar with its roots in the Beat era; upper floor customers have a prime view across the junction of Columbus Avenue and Broadway.*

Beat Landmarks

Painter and poet Lawrence Ferlinghetti was one of the founders of **City Lights**, 261 Columbus Avenue, the first all-paperback bookstore in the USA when it opened in 1953 and one that attracted lasting fame by publishing the first works by the Beat writers, making North Beach (albeit briefly) the literary epicentre of the USA. The shop continues to be an excellent general bookstore, as well as the perfect place to stock up on volumes by, and about, the major figures of the Beat era.

Close to City Lights, the graffiti-covered **Vesuvio**, 255 Columbus Avenue, opened in 1949, displays work by local artists on its walls. The bar provided a favourite rendezvous for Beat writers, who were sometimes joined by Welsh poet Dylan Thomas, a regular visitor to the area during his trips to San Francisco. In civic recognition of the Beats contribution to San Francisco life, the adjoining alley was renamed **Jack Kerouac Street** after the writer whose frenzied novel *On The Road*, partly written in a Pacific Heights loft, was one of Beat literature's lasting triumphs.

The Beats found inspiration in the wine and caffeine provided by North Beach's many cafés. One of the best, then and now, is **Caffe Trieste**, 609 Vallejo Street. Another enjoyable survivor is **Tosca**, 242 Columbus Avenue, its atmosphere enlivened by an opera-filled jukebox.

Telegraph Hill

The steep streets that lead away from North Beach rise swiftly into **Telegraph Hill**, named for the west coast's first telegraph station that was built here in 1853. With its stunning views across the bay and beyond, Telegraph Hill has become an expensive and exclusive residential neighbourhood. Dotted throughout are architecturally interesting homes, such as the streamlined modern apartment block at **1360 Montgomery Street,** seen in the 1947 film, *Dark Passage*, and the International style **Kahn House**, 66 Calhous Terrace, designed by Richard Neutra and completed in 1939.

Coit Tower ***

The real reason to make the vertiginous climb up Telegraph Hill, however, is **Coit Tower** (daily 10:00–18:00; open later in summer), the 210ft (64m) reinforced concrete column which stands at its summit. Named after Lillie Coit, who bequeathed $100,000 to the city on her death in 1929 on the understanding that it be spent 'for the purpose of adding to the beauty of the city I have always loved.' Coit Tower was completed in 1933.

More notable than the tower itself are the **murals** decorating the interior. During the Depression, a job creation scheme provided 25 unemployed artists with the brief to cover the tower's walls with depiction's of Californian scenes. The perceived communist sympathies in some of the murals (at a time of immense industrial strife in San Francisco) led to considerable controversy and caused the opening of the tower to be postponed. Best of the murals is Victor Arnautoff's *City Life*, portraying San Francisco's Financial District.

Left: *A 1957 statue of Christopher Columbus stands beside Coit Tower. Though the likeness is unintentional, the top of the tower is thought by many to resemble a fire-hose nozzle.*

Filbert and Greenwich Steps

It is not unusual in this city of 43 hills for streets to become pedestrian-only concrete or wooden steps for part of their length. Two of the most photogenic examples are the Filbert and Greenwich steps, which descend steeply from the east side of Telegraph Hill (close to Coit Tower) to Battery Street. The course of the Filbert Steps is marked by a plethora of shrubbery and several narrow lanes lined by tiny wooden cottages, some dating from the 1860s. Only slightly less scenic, the Greenwich Steps include on their course the playfully ramshackle exterior of the Julius Castle, a classy Italian restaurant since 1923.

(SS 383)

4
The Northern Waterfront

From souvenir shops selling cable-car key rings and 'I Love San Francisco' T-shirts to the sombre former jail cells of Alcatraz Island, the Northern Waterfront reveals San Francisco at its most varied.

With **Fisherman's Wharf**, the city cheekily encourages its most unsophisticated tourists to spend their time in cleverly created shopping centres and a string of amusements not unlike those in any seaside location. Nonetheless, the seagulls, street entertainers, and the delicious tang of saltwater in the air, all add to the area's undeniable appeal no matter how contrived it may sometimes seem. More importantly, Fisherman's Wharf is the embarkation point for the ferry to the not-to-be-missed **Alcatraz Island** and the restored and exceedingly well-documented buildings of the notorious former prison.

Elsewhere along the Northern Waterfront, the mood becomes appreciably less tacky and there are some fine collections of old ships and boats to be toured that serve to underscore San Francisco's maritime links. The Palace of Fine Arts is one of the city's strangest yet most compelling landmarks, while the splendid small museums of Fort Mason repay a few hours' investigation.

A tour along the Northern Waterfront culminates at San Francisco's greatest achievement, the **Golden Gate Bridge**. Reaching out from the city through vicious currents and tortuous winds to the rugged headlands of Marin County, the structure combines engineering ingenuity with an artist's sense of the beautiful, and often seems more like a miracle than a suspension bridge.

Don't Miss

****** Alcatraz Island:** the infamous former prison – excellent guided tours.
***** Exploratorium:** hands-on science exhibits that will amuse for hours.
***** Fort Mason Center:** wonderful museums and cultural organisations.
***** Golden Gate Bridge:** probably the world's most photogenic bridge.
**** Hyde Street Pier Historic Ships:** ageing sea vessels restored to working order and open for tours.
**** Palace of Fine Arts:** Bernard Maybeck's 'ruin'.

Opposite: *The USS Pampanito, moored at Fisherman's Wharf.*

DOMINGO GHIRARDELLI

Apprenticed to a confectioner in his native Italy, Domingo Ghirardelli emigrated to Peru where he met the eccentric James Lick, one of California's wealthiest men. Lick grew enamoured of Ghirardelli's chocolate and helped create a market for it in San Francisco. In 1849, Ghirardelli followed Lick to the city and established the chocolate factory that is now the shopping complex of Ghirardelli Square.

Fisherman's Wharf

In the early morning around Pier 49 it is still possible to steal a glimpse of fishermen unloading their catches from what was once a sizeable fishing fleet. Usually, however, few fishermen show their faces at Fisherman's Wharf, now the most tourist-orientated quarter of San Francisco. A few of Fisherman's Wharf's numbered piers are the points of departure for **ferries** to Alcatraz Island, Sausalito and Tiburon.

Attractions such as **Pier 39**, a collection of speciality shops, restaurants and amusements – including **Aquarium of the Bay** where visitors pass through a 300-foot-long acrylic tunnel, inside which swim some 10,000 creatures of the deep, before reaching many tanks holding Pacific Ocean denizens – set the generally unengaging tone. Off the west side of Pier 39, watch and listen for the colony of sea lions that took up residence here in the 1990s, inadvertently becoming a source of great human interest. Ambling around the souvenir shops and food stalls among roving street performers can provide an hour or two of innocent pleasure. In rain or with children to amuse, the likes of **Ripley's Believe It or Not! Museum,** 175 Jefferson Street, will amiably pass the time.

Some of the former industrial buildings of Fisherman's Warf have been imaginatively transformed into

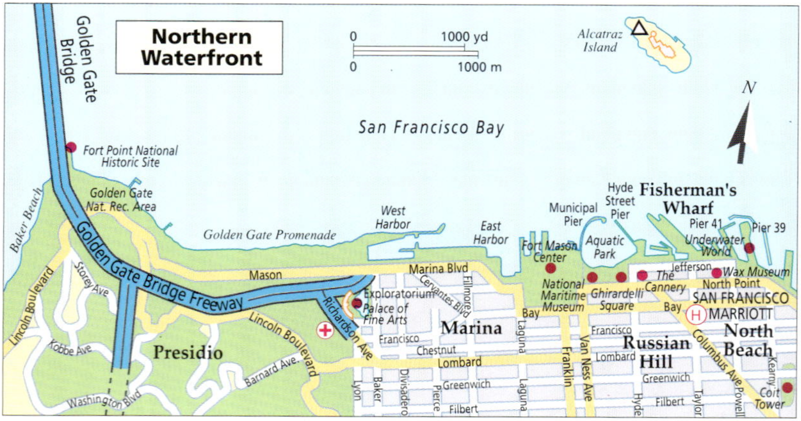

shopping and restaurant centres. One such is the old **Ghirardelli chocolate factory** (the Ghirardelli brand still a favourite indulgence of sweet-toothed San Franciscans; see panel), now **Ghirardelli Square**, 9800 N Point Street. Another complex meriting a look is the one-time fruit canning factory now known simply as **The Cannery**, 2801 Leavenworth Street.

To put some distance between yourself and the obvious tourist traps, walk to the gathering of top-notch nautical collections lying immediately west of Fisherman's Wharf. At **Hyde Street Pier Historic Ships** (mid-May–September daily 09:30–17:30; rest of the year daily 9:30–17:00) a fine gathering of restored vessels includes the 1890 *Eureka*, once the world's largest passenger ferry and the toast of Bay Area commuters, and the *Balcutha*, a mighty steel-hulled, square-rigged ship launched in 1886 that was no stranger to the dangers of rounding Cape Horn, as the explanatory texts on board emphasize.

Close by, the ship-shaped Art Deco form of the **National Maritime Museum**, 900 Beach Street (daily 10:00–17:00) holds an absorbing collection of seafaring paraphernalia, from massed figureheads to intricately detailed model ships.

San Francisco's role as a shipbuilding centre and a major embarkation point for troops in World War II, is remembered by two other nautical relics. Launched in 1943 and sinking 27,000 tons of enemy shipping, the submarine *USS Pampanito* can be boarded and its interior explored.

Above: *Aquatic Park overlooks the bay and the Hyde Street Pier Historic Ships collection.*
Opposite: *Aboard the Hawaiian Chieftain, one of Hyde Street Pier's ships.*

The Eagle Café

Fisherman's Wharf has seen many changes over the years but one item which still remains from the days when fishermen rather than tourists were its main visitors is the Eagle Café, serving wholesome meals and other refreshments since the 1920s. Now on the upper level of **Pier 39**, the rustic eatery originally stood two blocks away and was earmarked for demolition until public outrage saved its life. The original building was removed by crane and deposited in its current location in 1978. Serving food all day, the café also has live music in the evening.

Alcatraz Island

Just 1½ miles (2.4km) from Fisherman's Wharf is the island of Alcatraz, its diminutive size and proximity to the city (easily visible from almost any high point) belying its notorious reputation as the one-time site of the strictest and most feared prison in the USA. The west coast's first lighthouse was erected on Alcatraz in 1854 and the island saw use as a fort and military prison until the federal government took possession of it in 1934 to open the ultimate in maximum security jails – purpose-built to hold criminals deemed too dangerous and escape-prone to be held elsewhere.

The severity of the regime confirmed that Alcatraz was a place of punishment rather than rehabilitation. Prisoners were denied access to newspapers, radios and TVs, there was one guard for every three inmates, and work was regarded as a privilege that could only be earned through good behaviour.

The average stay at Alcatraz was 10 years yet only 80% of inmates ever received a visitor. Another torturous aspect was the fact that the sounds of San Francisco could be heard across the water – the clink of glasses at the yacht club's New Year's Eve party being particularly galling as the noise reverberated across the bay and into the cells. Of the 36 prisoners who attempted escape, all were recaptured within an hour, save for five who remain unaccounted for. Many presume the five to have drowned in the powerful currents and freezing waters of the bay, although rumours suggest otherwise; their breakout was dramatized in the 1979 film, *Escape from Alcatraz*.

Robert 'Birdman' Stroud

Though remembered as the 'Birdman of Alcatraz', murderer Robert Stroud began earning at least part of his nickname as an inmate of Leavenworth jail in Kansas. It was here that Stroud began keeping birds in his cell and where his studies of them led to his writing the highly regarded *Stroud's Digest of the Diseases of Birds*. Transferred to Alcatraz in 1942, Stroud was denied permission to keep birds in his cell. Nonetheless, *The Birdman of Alcatraz* was the title of a 1955 biography of him, as well as of a popular 1962 film starring Burt Lancaster as Stroud.

Among the 1576 convicts incarcerated during the prison's 29-year existence were infamous characters such as George 'Machine Gun' Kelly, Al Capone and Robert Stroud (the so-called 'Birdman of Alcatraz'). By the 1960s, however, the harshness of the regime was out of step with public opinion, and the growing number of minor criminals being sent to 'the Rock' caused great concern. This, coupled with the costs of running an island prison, contributed to the prison's closure in 1963. Left unoccupied, Alcatraz was reclaimed by a group of Native Americans for a period of two years beginning in 1969. Eventually, the island was declared part of the city's Golden Gate National Recreation Area and its features, such as the cellblock, exercise yard, and canteen, restored to provide the mainstay of public tours.

Tours ***

Alcatraz Island can only be reached by Blue and Gold Fleet ferry from Pier 41 at Fisherman's Wharf. The fare includes the loan of an audio cassette-guided tour once ashore. The tape unfurls a gripping commentary on the prison from ex-guards and a few embittered former inmates. Departures are at 30-minute intervals throughout the day and tickets go on sale at 08:00 (book a few days ahead in summer).

THE BATTLE OF ALCATRAZ

In May 1946, what became known as the Battle of Alcatraz erupted when Clarence Carnes, Marion Thompson, and Sam Shockley led other inmates in overpowering prison guards and seizing their weapons. The prison's complex system of security proved successful to some extent, however, as the prisoners failed to break through a second tier of guards and escape the cellblock. After the initial uprising, a standoff ensued for two days before order was restored. Two guards and three inmates lost their lives, as later did Shockley and Thompson, executed for their role in the escape attempt.

Left: *The garden at Alcatraz – behind the wall is the exercise yard of the notorious former prison.*
Opposite: *Alcatraz Island seen from Fisherman's Wharf, the water tower and the main buildings of the former prison clearly visible.*

Bernard Maybeck

Recognizing California's opportunities for inventive architecture, Bernard Maybeck, born in 1862 in New York but fresh from studying at the Ecole des Beaux Arts in Paris, settled in Berkeley in 1889. Becoming a familiar figure in his smock and beret, Maybeck wielded a considerable influence on Bay Area architecture. Though chiefly noted for his series of exuberant, rustic homes (many of which have sadly succumbed to forest fire) and the First Church of Christ Scientist in Berkeley (see p. 105), a different approach led to Maybeck's most enduring creation, the Palace of Fine Arts. The maverick architect died in 1957.

Opposite: *Warm colours of a Marina District house.*
Below: *The domed rotunda at the heart of the Palace of Fine Arts.*

Marina District

The Marina District, a spick-and-span neighbourhood of tastefully appointed family homes and high-rent, low-rise apartments, was built on landfill created for the 1915 Panama-Pacific Exposition. The purpose of the exposition was to celebrate the opening of the Panama Canal but more importantly, it symbolized San Francisco's recovery from the 1906 earthquake. The area's main commercial strip, **Chestnut Street**, is lined with chic shops and eateries that appeal to the generally well-off and fashionable residents of the area. Unfortunately for them, the Marina District is one of the San Francisco areas most prone to earthquake damage, due to its lack of solid foundations.

Fort Mason Center ***

Locally dubbed 'Fort Culture', Fort Mason Center is a symbol of San Francisco's support of creative endeavour with some 50 organizations making use of its low-rent offices and exhibition space, alongside theatres, a concert hall, and an award-winning vegetarian restaurant, all within the buildings of a former army barracks.

Fort Mason also houses several worthwhile museums which typically augment changing small displays drawn from their permanent holdings with more substantive temporary exhibitions. At the **Museum of Craft & Folk Art** (open Wednesday–Sunday 12:00–17:00) the subject matter can be anything from quilting to decoy ducks. Recent exhibitions have hilighted to the work of female tatooists, the art crafted from wood and bones found in the Nevada desert by artist Larry Williams, and the turned wooden bowls of the renowned California artist Bob Stocksdale.

The art of Italian-Americans – mostly from new artists living in the Bay Area – is the subject of **Museo Italo-Americano** (Wednesday-Sunday 12:00–17:00). Meanwhile, the work of contemporary black Californian artists is exhibited alongside a smattering of permanent displays at the **African American Historical and Cultural Society** (Wednesday-Sunday 12:00–17:00).

The **Mexican Museum**, which staged many notable exhibitions at Fort Mason until the year 2000, is due to open a purpose-built space in Yerba Buena Gardens during 2003.

Palace of Fine Arts **

Designed by the maverick Bay Area architect Bernard Maybeck (*see* p. 56) for the 1915 Panama-Pacific Exposition, the Palace of Fine Arts, at the west end of Lyon Street, was built to resemble a Roman ruin. Its 132ft (40m) domed rotunda is flanked by a fragmented colonnade and each group of columns is topped by weeping maidens and funeral urns. Maybeck's intention was for the palace to instil a sense of 'moderated sadness' as visitors passed through it on their way to view the Exposition's exhibition of classical art, then displayed in what is now the Exploratorium.

Exploratorium ***

A few relics of the Exposition are evident in the corners of the cavernous building that now holds the immensely popular Exploratorium, 3601 Lyon Street (Memorial Day–Labour Day daily 10:00–18:00; rest of the year Tuesday–Sunday 10:00–17:00, late opening every Wednesday to 21:00 or 21:30), where hundreds of hands-on exhibits explain the principles of the natural world to inquisitive minds. Children explore merrily for hours but adults, too, will find plenty to stimulate and entertain.

Fort Mason's Military Past

Originally part of San Francisco's Spanish *presidio*, founded in 1776, Fort Mason was first known as *Punto Mendanos* and then as *Black Point* following the US annexation of California. In 1882, the fort was renamed after **Colonel Richard Barnes Mason**, a former military governor of California. Fort Mason served as a key military base for the USA in several conflicts, beginning with the Spanish-American War of 1898 when it was used to move supplies to the Philippines. During World War II, Fort Mason was the main embarkation point for the Pacific war zone, with 1.5 million troops and 20 million tons of supplies passing through.

Golden Gate

Fort Point National Historic Site *

Overlooking the Golden Gate and completed in 1861, Fort Point and its battery of 126 cannons (manned by 600 soldiers) was built to defend San Francisco from seaborne attack. The brick-walled fortress could not withstand the onslaught of modern weaponry and was consequently abandoned in 1886. During World War II a 100-strong garrison used the fort as a base to guard a submarine net strung across the bay.

The fort is now preserved and protected as a national historic site and provides insights into 19th-century military life, with rooms lined by exhibits and park rangers in the role of Civil War-era soldiers leading informative guided tours.

Another good reason to visit the fort is simply for the unusual worm's-eye view it provides of the immense span of the Golden Gate Bridge.

Golden Gate Bridge Suicides

One unforeseen aspect of the Golden Gate Bridge was its instant popularity as a **suicide spot**, the first suicide taking place three months after its opening. Jumping from the bridge into the strong currents and freezing waters of the Golden Gate, and hitting the waves at 80mph (129kph), leaves virtually no chance of survival. Over 900 people are known to have leapt to their death from the bridge and the true figure is probably over a thousand. In 1993, city authorities decided to install special phones, linked directly to suicide counsellors, for the use of would-be jumpers with last-minute doubts.

Golden Gate Bridge ***

Rarely have 100,000 tons of steel been shaped into a form as aesthetically satisfying and as practical as the **Golden Gate Bridge**, which has provided a vital transport link between the city and Marin County since its completion in 1937. Seven miles (11km) long with towers as high as a 48-storey building, the bridge sees some 42 million vehicle crossings annually.

Prior to its construction, many in San Francisco believed that the swift currents and depth of the Golden Gate would render impossible the construction of a bridge across it. Nonetheless, official sanction for the project was acquired in 1930 and, in the midst of the Depression, a federal government bond issue of $35 million financed the structure.

The **opening** of the bridge was marked by a carnival-like mood in the city, with the ringing of church bells, the sounding of fog horns, and 200,000 people making the crossing on foot the day before the full opening permitted access to vehicles.

Officially, credit for the design is accorded to **Joseph Strauss**, a Chicago-based engineer who oversaw the construction of this and several hundred other suspension bridges around the world. Historians believe, however, that the real creativity was practised by Strauss's under-acknowledged backroom team. The distinctive reddish-orange **colour** of the bridge, formally known as International Orange, is regarded as the colour most distinguishable in fog. The fogs that frequently afflict the Golden Gate cast an evocative white shroud around the bridge. Painting the structure is a ceaseless task; work continues year-round with **5000 gallons (19,000 litres)** of paint being applied annually.

For the fullest sense of the structure's size, cross its 2-mile (3km) central span on foot – pedestrians are restricted to the eastern walkway (daily 05:00–21:00) – and peer down at the treacherous waters of the Golden Gate 220ft (67m) below as the wind whistles in your ears.

Opposite: *42 million crossings are made each year by car via the Golden Gate Bridge, many of them commuter traffic.*
Left: *The city seen through the struts of the Golden Gate Bridge from the Marin Headlands.*

SAN FRANCISCO'S OTHER BRIDGE

Magnificent though it is, the Golden Gate Bridge unfairly detracts from the excellence of the city's other major bridge, the **San Francisco-Oakland Bay Bridge** – informally known as the **Bay Bridge** and linking the city to the East Bay. A year older than the Golden Gate Bridge, the Bay Bridge became the world's longest steel structure on its 1936 completion. During one year of its three-year construction period, the Bay Bridge consumed 18% of all the steel produced in the US. Curiously, part of the bridge is actually a tunnel, its 8-mile route (12.9km) cutting through the bay island of Yerba Buena.

EWELRY
MANX HOTEL
CELLOR HOTEL
HERBERT
Marinello
BEAUTY TRAINING
SALE BOOKS
PUB
HOTEL STRAT
PHOTOLA
ICE CREA
STARLITE ROOF
ELLIS
25¢
DINNER

5
Nob Hill, Pacific Heights and Russian Hill

Simply put, **Nob Hill** means money. Rising high above the Financial District and forming a western boundary with Chinatown, Nob Hill's name derives from an Indian term, *nabob*, denoting a person of wealth and importance. The name became applicable during the late 1800s when the hilltop site became cluttered with the mansion homes of California's wealthiest people.

The mansions may be gone but Nob Hill is still lubricated by extreme wealth, demonstrated by the immaculately attired guests of its string of top-class hotels and by the moneyed San Franciscans who meet to gossip and do deals over lunch, dinner or a slap-up afternoon tea in the restaurants of the same hotels.

Pacific Heights has been housing the great and good almost as long as Nob Hill but unlike its neighbour, it still has many hundreds of sumptuous homes, almost all of them, it seems, having some degree of historical or architectural worth. A lengthy stroll through its streets provides plenty of surprises.

The creation of Nob Hill was directly linked to the birth of the cable car and there is no better place to familiarize yourself with the intricacies of this unique form of transportation than at the Cable Car Museum.

While much is made of Lombard Street's steep gradient and corkscrew shape as it passes through the neighbourhood, **Russian Hill** is overlooked by many visitors. This leafy residential has few obvious attractions yet it comes as close as anywhere in San Francisco to epitomising the city's mood of cultured relaxation.

DON'T MISS

** **Cable Car Museum:** the inside story on the city's famous cable cars.
** **Grace Cathedral:** among the city's most impressive church interiors.
** **Lombard Street:** San Francisco's much photographed crookedest street.
** **Macandray Lane:** the city's most peaceful and picturesque street.
*** **Nob Hill:** the neighbourhood of the ultra-wealthy.
** **Pacific Heights:** from mansions to eight-sided dwellings, full of surprises.

Opposite: *Nob Hill rises high above the Financial District.*

> **The Masonic Temple and Auditorium**
>
> One of the most striking buildings on Nob Hill is the Masonic Temple and Auditorium, 1111 California Street. The white marble building, constructed in the 1950s, is decorated with bas-reliefs representing the armed forces and honouring those masons who died during wartime service. American freemasonry being considerably less secretive than its counterparts elsewhere in the world, the building can be entered to admire the huge window (depicting an apron-clad mason) and the masonic eye, that looms above the lobby. The 3000-seat auditorium has a regular programme of concerts and theatrical events.

Nob Hill

The invention of the cable car in 1873 made accessible one of San Francisco's biggest hills, the 338ft (103m) Nob Hill. Convenient for the Financial District, Nob Hill immediately drew California's inordinately wealthy railroad barons, including Charles Crocker, Mark Hopkins, Collis P Huntington and Leland Stanford – the so-called 'Big Four' who made their fortunes initially through the gold rush (*see* p. 15). Each lavished millions of dollars on spectacular palatial abodes; in so doing, they cemented Nob Hill's reputation as a haunt of the very rich and very powerful.

Peek into the sumptuous public rooms of any of the four luxury hotels on Nob Hill today – the Fairmont, with its plush lobby, the Huntington, the Stanford Court, and the Mark Hopkins, offering fabulous views – to see that Nob Hill still sees its share of the good life. The hotels arose from the ashes of the original mansions, all but one having been destroyed in the fire that followed the earthquake in 1906. The only survivor (thanks to its sandstone construction) was the **Flood Mansion**, completed for silver-mining millionaire James Flood in 1886. The mansion is now home to the exclusive and highly secretive gentlemen-only **Pacific Union Club**.

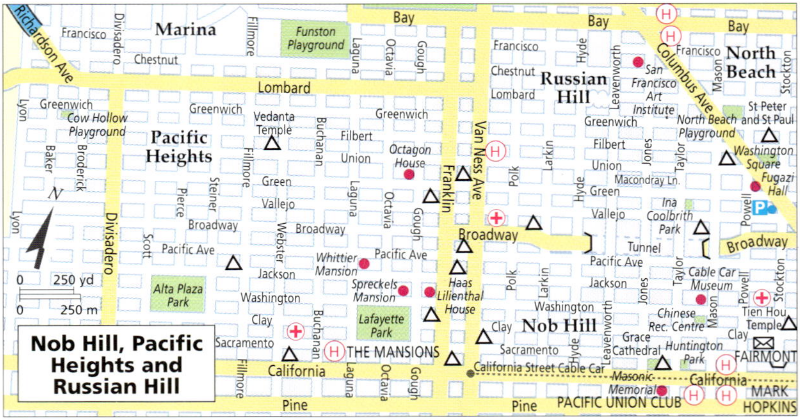

Grace Cathedral **

In a neighbourhood resonant with material excesses, **Grace Cathedral**, 1051 Taylor Street, provides a stylish spiritual sanctuary. The Episcopalian cathedral, modelled on Notre Dame in Paris and raised on the site of Charles Crocker's mansion, was begun in 1928 but a series of delays caused the consecration to be as late as 1964.

At the main entrance, the **Doors of Paradise** are gilded bronze portals decorated with biblical scenes moulded from the Lorenzo Ghiberti doors of the Baptistry in Florence. Above, the stunning **rose window** was the work of Gabriel Loire in Chartres. Inside, a 15th-century French altarpiece and exquisite Flemish reredos adorn the **Chapel of Grace**, while the series of stained-glass windows depict biblical scenes and human achievers as diverse as Albert Einstein, Henry Ford and Frank Lloyd Wright.

Opposite Grace Cathedral's main entrance, **Huntington Park** is a small but relaxing open space – a perfect green spot from which to watch the well-heeled of Nob Hill go about their business and the Chinese from nearby Chinatown stretching through their t'ai chi exercises.

Above: *One of the city's many trusty cable cars, on Hyde Street.*

The Cable Car Museum **

An appropriate adjunct to a tour of Nob Hill is a visit to the nearby **Cable Car Museum**, 1201 Mason Street (April-September daily 10:00–18:00; October-March daily 10:00–17:00) and its excellent collection of ageing cable cars and related memorabilia. On the lower level is the creaking winding gear used to keep the 11 miles (17.7km) of steel wire pulling the city's 38 cable cars moving at a steady speed of 9½mph (15kmph).

Nob Hill Mansions

The first to build big and spectacular on Nob Hill was **Leland Stanford**, who raised an Italianate villa in 1876. The interior included a two-storey rotunda. The $3-million **Mark Hopkins** pile went up a few years later, an over-elaborate architectural mishmash built to the wild imaginings of Hopkins' wife. **Charles Crocker's** home cost a comparatively modest $2.3 million but boasted a million-dollar art collection. Crocker increased his infamy by erecting a 'spite fence' to deny sunlight to a neighbour who refused to sell his land.

Cow Hollow's Rise and Fall

Pacific Heights used to contain freshwater springs and grassy meadows. By the 1860s, a section around a natural lagoon had come to be known as Cow Hollow as it held the dairy farms that supplied the city with its cheese, fresh milk and later meat. Cow Hollow became increasingly attractive to wealthy settlers unimpressed by farm noises and smells. City authorities bowed to mounting public pressure and, in 1891, banned the ownership of livestock and filled in the lagoon.

Pacific Heights

Spread across several hills and boasting fabulous views of the bay, Pacific Heights is a coveted residential address. Since the late 19th century, it has been home to many of San Francisco's most important and affluent people. Invitingly, the mostly quiet residential streets see comparatively few tourists but justify exploration for the preponderance of buildings noted for their architecture or simply their opulence.

Pacific Heights has a strong reputation for shopping, but don't expect any bargains. Along the 1700–2000 blocks of Union Street are fashionable outlets for costly European designer clothing and valuable antiques, and speciality shop after speciality shop dispensing the oddments that trendy locals feel they cannot live without. Union Street shopping is done in an atmosphere of cultivated quaintness as many retail outlets occupy 19th-century buildings raised by farmers (the area was once known as Cow Hollow for its many dairy farms).

Below: *Delivery van on Union Street in tranquil Pacific Heights.*

Above: *A North Beach hairdresser which caters to the stars.*

Pacific Heights on Foot **

While some of its gradients may be daunting, Pacific Heights has plenty to repay a few hours' exploration on foot. A good place to start, if only because everything else is downhill in relation to it, is **Lafayette Park**. Bordered by Sacramento, Washington, Gough and Laguna streets, at 378ft (115m) Lafayette Park is not only the highest point in Pacific Heights but also the greenest, with some 13 acres (5.2ha) of trees, tidy lawns and colourful flower beds. Curiously, the park had a large house, **Holladay's Heights**, in its centre from 1868 to 1936, erected by a former attorney and the subject of a long-running legal battle over an individual's right to build in a public park.

Views from the park – be they of the bay in the distance or of the elegant homes which encircle it – are stunning. Similarly eye-catching is the beaux-arts **Spreckels Mansion**, facing the park at 2080 Washington Street. The most elegant home in Pacific Heights, the mansion dates from 1912 and was built for Adolph Spreckels, colossally rich through his family's sugar-refining empire, and his wife, Alma. A prominent San Francisco couple, the Spreckels founded the California Palace of the Legion of Honor (*see* pp. 95–96).

In keeping with many Pacific Heights homes, the Spreckels Mansion is a private dwelling and not open to the public. One imposing structure that can be entered, however, is the **Haas Lilienthal House**, 2007 Franklin Street. Excellent guided tours (Wednesday 12:00–15:00; Sunday 11:00–16:00) outline the story of the Haas and Lilienthal families, who occupied this three-storey home for 86 years, and reveals room after room decorated in period style. The house is also the headquarters of the Foundation for San Francisco's Architectural Heritage; many useful books and pamphlets on the city's history are on sale in the foyer.

The Spreckels Family

A fortune built on sugar refining enabled Prussian-born **Claus Spreckels** to be one of the wealthiest people in post-Gold Rush San Francisco. Expanding into transportation and the provision of gas and electricity, the Spreckels fortunes were increased by Claus's four sons, though feuding was rife among them, and between them and their father. In 1884, the Spreckels clashed with another prominent family, the **De Youngs**. After the De Young-owned *San Francisco Examiner* published allegations that the Spreckels' company had defrauded shareholders, Adolph Spreckels shot and wounded M H de Young. The interfamily rivalry extended to the city's two major art museums (*see* pp. 87 and 95).

The Swedenborgian Church

Several noted Bay Area architects, foremost among them **Arthur Page Brown** and **Bernard Maybeck**, contributed to the design of the Swedenborgian Church, on the western edge of Pacific Heights at 2107 Lyon Street. Completed in 1894, the log-cabin-like church reflects the impact of the turn-of-the-century Arts and Crafts Movement and the influence of Swedenborgianism itself, using nature to express the human soul. Inside, the fireplace and rough-hewn wood beams are Californian timber, as is the hand-crafted furniture.

Substantially smaller than the Haas Lilienthal House but no less interesting, the 1861 **Octagon House**, 2645 Gough Street (open second Wednesday and second and fourth Sundays of the month, except during January, 12:00–15:00) was one of five eight-sided wooden homes built in San Francisco. The octagonal shape serves no practical purpose but was considered lucky by the house's owners. Restored by the National Society of Colonial Dames (an organization founded in 1891 to preserve the heritage of the US's colonial period), the house now stages temporary exhibitions of colonial- and Federal-period decorative art.

The city's other surviving Octagon House (no public admission) stands at 1067 Green Street, neighboured by several other contrasting but architecturally interesting homes. Demonstrating the diversity of San Franciscan taste, the houses here range from the English Tudor appearance of number 1088 to the Southwestern Pueblo style of number 1030.

For sheer madcap exuberance, however, few Pacific Heights buildings come close to matching the **Vedanta Temple** at the junction of Webster and Filmore streets. A dizzying confection of domes, turrets and Moorish features, the temple was completed in 1908 for a Hindu sect. In the belief that all religions lead eventually to God, the temple encouraged tolerance and peacefulness and found sympathy amid the materially satisfied but sometimes spiritually unfulfilled inhabitants of Pacific Heights.

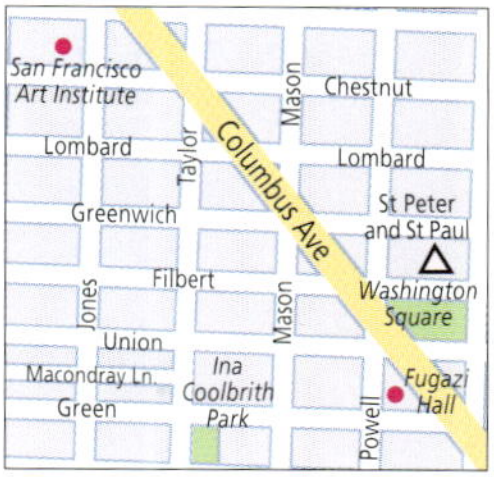

Russian Hill

A cultured community studded with 19th-century shingled homes and quiet, tree-lined lanes leading off extremely steep streets, Russian Hill was the beat of San Francisco's earliest bohemia and has evolved into a wealthy residential district. The click of tourists' cameras only disturbs the peace along the section of **Lombard Street** between Hyde and Leavenworth streets. Here, the 27° gradient – landscaped during the 1920s into a series of curves, decorated by plants and bushes – is navigated by a procession of vehicles observing the 5mph (8kmph) speed limit as they make their giddy, corkscrewing descent.

The neighbourhood's creative energies are evinced by the oldest art school on the west coast, the **San Francisco Art Institute**, 800 Chestnut Street. The Institute moved into these premises – intended to resemble a medieval monastery – in 1926. Student art decorates the corridors and galleries but the main attraction is the **Diego Rivera Gallery**, named after the great Mexican muralist who taught here for a spell in the 1930s and whose piece, showing a mural being painted and including a rear-view image of Rivera himself, decorates one wall.

Probably the prettiest Russian Hill side street is **Macondray Lane**, running for just two blocks between Union and Green streets and accessible via a wooden staircase rising from Taylor Street. After viewing the lane, continue to **Ina Coolbrith Park** at the junction of Vallejo and Taylor streets. A pocket of rampant vegetation, the park is named after a Russian Hill resident who, in 1919, became California's first poet laureate.

Opposite: *A section of much photographed Lombard Street.*
Below: *Lombard Street's strict speed limit is there for a purpose.*

The Naming of Russian Hill

Russian Hill is believed to have been named after a group of Russian sailors (thought to be linked to a Russian fur-trapping settlement on California's northern coast) who were buried in an informal grave site at the crest of Vallejo Street, probably in the early 1800s. One story tells that children playing around the graves in the mid-1800s began referring to the area as Russian Hill.

6
Civic Center, SoMa, Mission District and The Castro

Before being outshone by the Financial District and, more recently, by Yerba Buena Gardens, the **Civic Center** was regarded as the architectural showcase of San Francisco. In the wake of the 1906 earthquake and fire, the Civic Center was conceived to please the eye as well as provide a new seat of local government. The beaux-arts style complex reaches its climax in the stunning City Hall.

South across Market Street, a much more recent spate of building has seen the **SoMa** neighbourhood transformed from an industrial wasteland into the stylishly sculptured complex of arts venues and museums that form Yerba Buena Gardens. No single place is more pleasing for its architecture or its contents than the new, purpose-built San Francisco Museum of Modern Art, a source of considerable civic pride and deservedly so.

Moving west, the **Mission District** grew around Mission Dolores, the oldest building in the city and a rare reminder of San Francisco's Spanish colonial era – the District's current population is largely Spanish speaking, drawn from Central and South America. While in the neighbourhood, anyone who has ever worn a pair of jeans might be intrigued to visit the Levi Strauss Factory at 250 Valencia Street, opened by the man who invented jeans in San Francisco as hardwearing trousers for gold miners.

Immediately west of the Mission District, the **Castro** is a celebrated gay and lesbian area where the many freedoms enjoyed today – in what looks like any other affluent residential neighbourhood – were won through community action.

Don't Miss

**** Ansel Adams Center for Photography:** acclaimed, world-class exhibitions.
***** Asian Art Museum:** large and diverse stock of Asian treasures.
***** City Hall:** an architecturally glorious base for city government, resplendent beneath its green dome.
**** Mission Dolores:** the oldest building in the city and the first European toe-hold on San Francisco.
***** San Francisco Museum of Modern Art:** an innovative home for a substantial stock of modern art.

Opposite: *Yerba Buena Gardens is the heart of SoMa (South of Market).*

Civic Center

As San Francisco's administrative centre and the site of its major concert and opera venues, **Civic Center** is a mixture of accomplished recent building and dreamy beaux-arts structures that arose from the debris of the 1906 earthquake and fire. The attractive complex is dominated by **City Hall**, its green copper dome visible across much of San Francisco. Enter this delightful building, which has held the cogs of the municipal machine since its 1915 completion, climb the grand marble staircase and stroll the corridors, vibrant with arches, porticoes and neoclassical sculptures.

Behind City Hall, the graceful **War Memorial Opera House** (opened in 1932) was inspired by Garnier's *Opera* in Paris. September's gala **opening night** of the opera season brings a rare opportunity to observe San Francisco's high society bedecked in all its finery, but tickets are hard to come by unless you have good connections.

The neighbouring **Louise M Davies Symphony Hall** is the forthright glass and granite home of the San Francisco Philharmonic Orchestra. Completed in 1981, the hall's scandalously poor sound quality caused it to be closed for a $10 million acoustical refurbishment. It was reopened to great acclaim in 1991.

The formal landscaping of **Civic Center Plaza** lies opposite City Hall's main entrance, with the **former San Francisco Public Library** on its eastern side. The elegant 1915 library now houses the outstanding Asian Art Museum (*see* panel) while its million-plus books and historical paraphernalia, the raw material for numerous engaging exhibitions, are now within the state-of-the-art confines of the **new public library**, at the junction of Grove and Hyde streets.

The Jukebox Marriott

One addition to SoMa, which by and large has failed to win San Franciscan hearts, is the Marriott Hotel, 777 Market Street. Filling the entire plot between Market and Mission streets, the hotel rises for 39 storeys and is topped by a combined bar and observation level. The hotel's abundance of glass, seen at its best when reflecting the setting sun, encouraged San Francisco's long-serving newspaper columnist **Herb Caen** to dismissively label it the 'juke-box Marriott' following its completion in 1989.

Opposite: *War Memorial Opera House, home of the city's leading opera company.*

SoMa

In 1981, the opening of the $200-million **Moscone Convention Center** signalled the beginning of a major transformation of **SoMa**. Long established as an industrial area holding the city's rail freight yards, SoMa by the 1970s was a largely derelict plot of warehouses and factories that was abandoned when the city's cargo terminals were relocated. Attracted by low rents and spacious light-filled interiors, aspiring artists colonized some of the old buildings, sometimes selling their work through the art galleries that soon appeared in the neighbourhood, swiftly followed by a clutch of nightclubs and bars.

The 1980s saw SoMa's steady gentrification. Rents rose and many of the old buildings were transformed into luxury apartments or offices favoured by computer and media companies. Even more dramatic was the steady construction of **Yerba Buena Gardens**, an ambitious work-in-progress arts and cultural complex that is making SoMa an integral part of San Francisco life.

The Asian Art Museum

Now with treasures spanning 6000 years and drawn from Asia's religions, countries and cultures, the Asian Art Museum first opened in 1966 to display the collections of industrialist Avery Brundage. The **Chinese galleries** reflect Brundage's main area of interest and are a feast of jades, porcelains and calligraphy from several dynasties. Elsewhere are marvellous Japanese Edo-period screen paintings, a wonderful stash of 18th- and 19th-century netsuke, and Hindu, Buddhist and Jain sculptures dominating the **Indian** galleries.

Jack London's Birthplace

Many internationally known writers have lived in San Francisco but relatively few have actually been born in the city. One exception is Jack London, author of short stories and novels such as *Call of the Wild* and *The Sea Wolf*, born in SoMa in 1876. London spent little time in San Francisco, moving to Oakland as a child and later building a farmhouse in northern California's Sonoma Valley, but he's still remembered by a **plaque** at **615 Third Street**. The plaque marks the site of London's birth, though some believe it was elsewhere in SoMa and long since demolished.

Yerba Buena Gardens ***

A 12-block area enclosed by Market, Harrison, Second, and Fifth streets, Yerba Buena Gardens is the home of the new **San Francisco Museum of Modern Art** (*see* pp. 74–75) and of the **Center for the Arts**, a $44-million venue boasting state-of-the-art film, theatre, and performances spaces, plus well-equipped visual arts galleries. Outside, an appealingly landscaped 5-acre (2ha) park – scene of lunchtime concerts and poetry readings – is traversed by the **Esplanade** walkway and lined by terraced cafés.

Such has been the success of Yerba Buena Gardens that many of the city's museums and institutions have moved, or plan to move, into the area. Another arrival has been the Sony **Metreon**, filling a large plot on the corner of Mission and Fourth streets with cinemas, an IMAX theatre, countless shops and state-of-the-art inter-active attractions.

Longer established is the outstanding **Ansel Adams Center for Photography**, 655 Mission Street (Tuesday-Sunday 11:00–17:00; open until 20:00 first Thursday of the month), founded by and named after the San Francisco-born photographer famed for his evocative images of the US's national parks and natural areas.

A small gallery displays selections from a collection of 125 Adams photographs – a mixture of his classic nature studies and lesser-known pieces spanning his entire career – but the primary purpose of the space is the mounting of temporary exhibitions showcasing the most accomplished, most challenging photography from around the world.

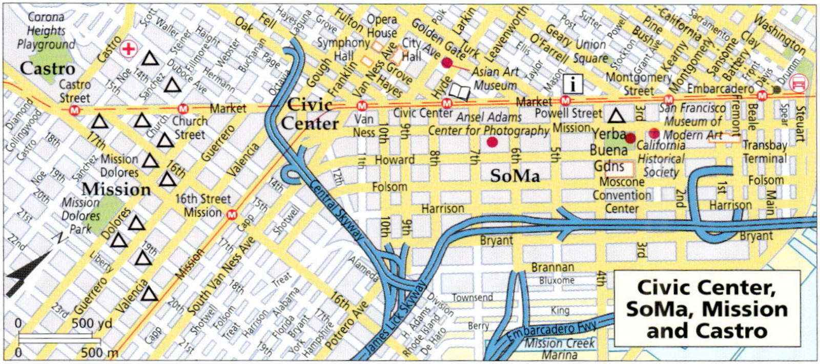

Housed in a petite wood-framed building that opened as a hardware store in 1918, the **California Historical Society**, 678 Mission Street (for times, tel: (415) 567 1848) provides an invaluable resource to the serious researcher wishing to delve into the minutiae of California's past. For the merely curious, there are periodic exhibitions drawn from the society's immense stock of historical artefacts and its collection of 19th-century Californian art.

A very different kind of art is the stock-in-trade of the **Cartoon Art Museum**, 1017 Market Street (Tuesday-Friday 11:00–17:00, Sunday 13:00–17:00), one of three museums in the USA preserving and displaying cartoon art. The changing exhibitions explore aspects of the history and creation of cartoons, revealing the intricacies and skills of this under-acknowledged art form.

In a handsome 1920s high-rise building at odds with the new construction all around it, the **Telephone Pioneer Communications Museum**, 140 New Montgomery Street (Monday-Friday 10:00–15:00), occupies the ground floor of the Pacific Telephone Building. Getting messages to and around California in the Gold Rush era was far from easy. This entertaining clutter, which includes ungainly old phones and telegraph machines, examines these difficulties and comes bang up to date by explaining the wonders of satellites and fibre-optic cable.

Opposite: *The eccentric landscaped pathways of Yerba Buena Gardens.*

SoMa Shopping

Before it became a centre for cultural pursuits, SoMa was known to San Franciscans mainly for its scores of **factory discount outlets**, offering clothing and other goods at much less than normal retail price. Many discount stores remain and are widely advertised in newspapers and on leaflets found all over the city. Whether seeking shoes, raincoats, umbrellas or bathroom scales, shoppers can typically make savings of up to 40% on normal prices. Many well-known clothing designers have their own outlets here, and there is a worthwhile multi-store centre at **Yerba Buena Square**, 899 Howard Street.

Above: *The striking interior of the San Francisco Museum of Modern Art.*

San Francisco Museum of Modern Art

Notable for its design as well as for its excellent collection of art, sculpture, photography and more, **San Francisco Museum of Modern Art**, 151 Third Street (summer Sunday-Tuesday, Friday and Saturday 10:00–18:00, Thursday 10:00–21:00; rest of the year Sunday-Tuesday and Thursday-Saturday 11:00–18:00) is the stunning $60-million centrepiece of the Yerba Buena Gardens complex. Opened in 1995, the inspired building is hard to miss – a black-and-white striped cylinder sprouts from its tiered brickwork, helping to maximize the natural light reaching the interior spaces.

THE MUSEUM'S FORMER HOME

First-time visitors to the San Francisco Museum of Modern Art will find it hard to imagine the cramped space that the museum previously occupied. Founded in 1935, the museum earned considerable acclaim through the 1940s by staging the first solo exhibitions by the emerging names of abstract expressionism. But the poorly lit rooms and corridors of the War Memorial's **Veterans' Building**, in Civic Center, struggled to remain a suitable home as the permanent collections grew. The opening of the current museum in 1995 enabled San Francisco to regain the upper hand over Los Angeles as the west coast's premier space for 20th-century art.

American art

Fittingly for a museum that established itself in the 1940s (albeit in less salubrious premises) with a groundbreaking exhibition of abstract expressionism, it is artists associated with this genre that contribute some of the most spectacular canvases in the collection. Jackson Pollock's *Guardians of the Secret* stands out, as do diverting pieces from Pollock's New York School contemporaries such as Willem de Kooning and Barnett Newman. Look out, too, for the special side galleries displaying works donated by the underrated Californian, Clyfford Still, and the intriguing Bay Area artist Richard Diebenkorn.

From Georgia O'Keeffe to Andy Warhol, most luminaries of modern American art are represented, and there is a strong contingent from Latin America, including Frida Kahlo and Diego Rivera, whose contributions include the often reproduced *Flower Carrier*. Among recent works are provocative pieces from Jeff Koons, Cindy Sherman and Sol LeWitt.

European art

A broad and impressive documentation of the major names and movements of 20th-century European art reaches its climax with the bright, exploding colours of Matisse's *Woman with the Hat*. There are also significant Cubist offerings, such as Picasso's *Head in Three-quarter View* and *The Coffee Pot*, and Braque's *Violin and Candlestick*; and an excellent selection of German Expressionism, featuring a strong contribution from Max Beckmann and a large collection of drawings by Paul Klee. Salvador Dali and Max Ernst are among the major names represented in the galleries devoted to surrealist canvases.

Architecture and design

The paintings may justifiably hold the attention of most visitors, but there is much to be enjoyed in the galleries devoted to architecture and design. Historical exhibits feature notable California and Bay Area figures such as Bernard Maybeck and Willis Polk, both active locally from the late 1800s. The collection spans the Pacific Rim and includes, among many others, the futuristic furniture of Japan's Shiro Kuramata.

Photography

With selections from the museum's 14,000 photographs shown on rotation, the third-floor photography galleries provide an exceptionally good guide to the rise of the medium through the 20th century. Pioneering work by Europeans, such as Man Ray, Moholy-Nagy and Atget, is liable to feature strongly and serves to complement the American modernists such as Bernice Abbot, Walker Evans and Edward Steichen.

MARIO BOTTA: THE MUSEUM'S ARCHITECT

San Francisco's Museum of Modern Art was the first museum project for Swiss architect Mario Botta and his first building in the USA. Recipient of numerous awards and widely credited with reviving modernist architecture, Botta earned a strong reputation for fusing modernist forms with great sensitivity to human needs. Strongly influenced by Le Corbusier and Louis I Kahn (noted architects with whom he worked as a student) Botta's other constructions have included a cathedral in France, an art gallery in Tokyo and administrative buildings in South Korea.

Below: *Horizontal bands on pillars and walls catch the eye at the entrance to the Museum of Modern Art.*

THE LEVI STRAUSS FACTORY

Built following the 1906 earthquake and fire, the Levi Strauss Factory, 250 Valencia Street in the Mission District, is the home of the world-famous jeans invented by Levi Strauss (a Bavarian-born San Francisco merchant) and Jacob Davis (a Nevada tailor) to provide hard-wearing trousers for gold miners, with riveted seams and pockets sufficiently strong for holding tools. Although the garments became known as 'jeans', Strauss preferred to call them 'waist-high overalls'. Once a month, the factory can be visited on an informative guided tour; reservation are necessary, tel: (415) 565–9159.

MISSION DISTRICT

Its thick adobe walls providing protection against earthquakes, **Mission Dolores**, 320 Dolores Street (daily 08:00–12:00 and 13:00–16:00), is the oldest building in San Francisco. Founded in 1776, it lends its name to the Latin-American-dominated Mission District.

The mission's tiny **chapel** resonates with history. The gilded altar piece dates from 1780, the bells and wooden statues come from 19th-century Mexico and many of the wooden beams are original. Yet the chapel's modest proportions reflect the fact that the San Francisco mission – one of 21 raised by the Spanish as they colonized California – never enjoyed particular importance.

The mission's past is superficially outlined in the **museum**. Outside, the well-tended cemetery is believed to have held the remains of some 5000 neophytes – Native Americans converted to Christianity. Many of the earliest tomb markers no longer survive, though the oldest headstones remember notables of the post-Spanish *Californio* era.

War-time work in factories and shipyards drew a major influx of **Latin Americans** to San Francisco during the 1940s, many settling in the Mission District. The population has steadily expanded and includes many Mexicans, Guatemalans, Costa Ricans, Nicaraguans and Salvadoreans, with smaller enclaves of Bolivians, Colombians, Peruvians and Chileans. Besides countless Latin-American restaurants and bakeries, the Mission District is noted for its **murals**, the best concentration of which are in and around Balmy Alley, between 24th and 25th streets, near Harrison Street.

During the late 1990s, an influx of internet entrepreneurs (dubbed 'the dot.commers') into Mission District homes caused much local resentment as rents rose and many long-established residents were forced out of the city. Few tears were shed when the e-commerce economy collapsed in 2001.

Opposite: *Palm-studded Mission Dolores Park lies just south of Mission Dolores chapel.*
Below: *Live music is a feature of the Mission District.*

THE CASTRO

Since the 1970s, there have been few better places to be gay or lesbian than San Francisco's once neglected now prosperous Castro neighbourhood.

A spick-and-span district of lovingly maintained Victorian homes and businesses owned by, and catering largely to, the area's predominantly gay and lesbian population, the Castro was the base from which the city's long-established gay community collectively and provocatively came out. Through a series of confrontations with police and numerous political breakthroughs, San Francisco's gays and lesbians became a powerful section of the city's population and an inspiration to gay people worldwide.

Several landmarks in San Francisco's gay history are to be found along **Castro Street**, including the raised pavement outside the Bayview Bank where local camera-shop owner Harvey Milk began the campaign that would make him the USA's first openly gay person to be elected to public office. Notice too the bars and restaurants that broke with the tradition of hiding their clientele in dimly lit interiors by installing large windows along the street, and the rainbow flags of gay solidarity hanging from many buildings.

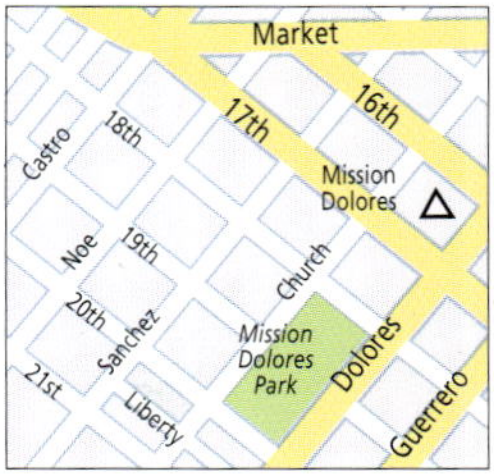

THE CASTRO THEATRE

Completed in 1923, the sumptuous Castro Theatre looms large on Castro Street. While the cinema predates the gay settlement of the neighbourhood, it has been adopted by the local community and, alongside a programme of mainstream and cult films, hosts the **Gay and Lesbian Film Festival** each June.

THE NAMES PROJECT QUILT

Started in 1987 to allow a lover, relative or friend of a victim of Aids to express their grief and remember their lost one by weaving a quilt in their honour, the Names Project Quilt, 2362 Market Street, now comprises tens of thousands of individually hand-woven quilts. Sections of the quilt have been carried to world capitals to draw attention to the high death toll from Aids and protest government indifference to the crisis.

7
Haight-Ashbury and Golden Gate Park

Many San Francisco neighbourhoods have topsy-turvy histories but few have experienced ups and downs as spectacular as **Haight-Ashbury**. Created in the 1880s to coincide with the opening of Golden Gate Park, the area acquired a feast of elegant Victorian houses that later provided an unlikely backdrop to the 1967 hippie invasion known as the 'Summer of Love'. From the mid-1990s, the neighbourhood's social star has been ascending, with expensive renovation work, new shops and restaurants beginning to evoke the flavour of the well-to-do Haight-Ashbury of a 100 years ago.

The 19th-century building styles range from the San Franciscan Stick style to fanciful Queen Anne, punctuated here and there by Italianate and other pseudo-European forms. Impossibly large bay windows, turrets and towers are features of houses lining almost every street.

The spectacular 1960s brought the neighbourhood international fame but masked the growing dilapidation of the old houses, while the low-income population faced the urban pressures that led to the area's social decline. By the 1980s, a community effort to reduce crime and hard-drug use enjoyed success, while widespread renovation of the old homes has improved the atmosphere without diminishing Haight-Ashbury's place at the forefront of San Francisco's alternative culture.

To the west, **Golden Gate Park** is a beautiful green space of overwhelming proportions. Tour it by bike or roller-skates, and allow time for an excellent art museum and the California Academy of Sciences.

Don't Miss

***** Golden Gate Park:** enormous, famous and inviting, it holds everything a city park should and a lot more besides.
***** Haight-Ashbury:** wonderful Victorian homes characterize this effervescent neighbourhood that was at the very heart of 1960s hippiedom.
***** MH De Young Museum:** an absorbing collection of mostly American art, from the early days of European settlement to the present.

Opposite: *An impressively maintained Victorian house in Haight-Ashbury.*

> **Dividing Haight-Ashbury**
>
> In the 1860s, most of what became Haight-Ashbury and Golden Gate Park was officially known as the Outside Lands, 17,000 acres (6880ha) of scrubland and sand dunes between the western edge of the then city and the ocean. Squatters living in shacks claimed chunks of the undeveloped land, though many were paid to do so by wealthy speculators who recognized the area's potential. As the speculators exploited their political connections, a deal was struck which gave the squatters legal ownership of 90% of the land, the rest going to the city for the building of Golden Gate Park.

Haight-Ashbury

Its name writ large in America's counter-culture, **Haight-Ashbury** was the destination for an estimated 75,000 long-haired youths in psychedelic garb from all over the USA who arrived in 1967 for what became known as the **Summer of Love**, perhaps the definitive few months of the hippie movement. Most were drawn by a utopian dream of a free and easy lifestyle with no need for money, a regular supply of soft drugs and music performed for free by neighbourhood bands such as the **Grateful Dead** and **Jefferson Airplane**. For many the dream soon turned to a nightmare as sheer numbers turned Haight-Ashbury into a ghetto where crime, hard-drug use and disease – encouraged by unhealthy diets, walking barefoot and rampant libidos – became rife.

The origins of Haight-Ashbury (named for two major streets) during the 1880s were as a weekend retreat for well-to-do San Franciscans. The area was developed from scrub after a new cable-car line linked it to the city proper, providing transport to the Golden Gate Park.

Far enough west of the city centre to be spared the destructive fire that followed the 1906 earthquake, Haight-Ashbury still has many of **Victorian houses** from its earliest days, providing a wonderful visual record of changing San Francisco building styles and residential tastes since the turn of the 20th century.

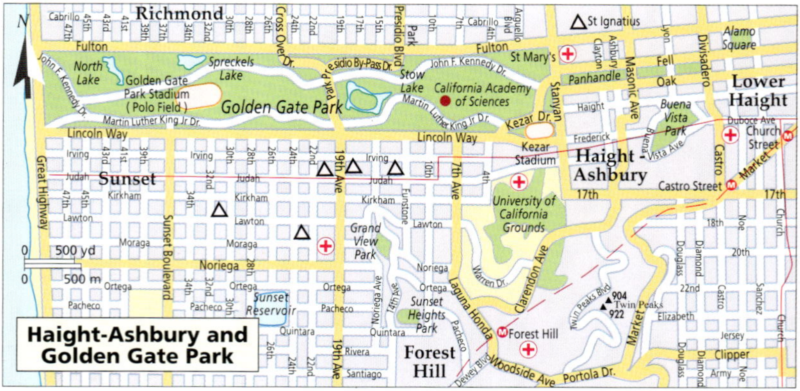

Haight-Ashbury and Golden Gate Park

A few years before the invasion of 1967, Haight-Ashbury had been in the throes of a small-scale, but very genuine, social revolution. Seen by some as a continuation of the Beat culture that emerged in 1950's North Beach, it was greatly aided by the neighbourhood's low rents as many of the graceful Victorian homes were run-down and divided into apartments, which made it accessible to an anarchic mixture of ageing Beats, creative misfits, and students from the nearby San Francisco University. Many were experimenting with the hallucinogenic drug **LSD** (legal until 1966 and in plentiful supply), performing avant-garde theatre, and organising free music in Haight-Ashbury's streets and open spaces. On the neighbourhood's main commercial artery of **Haight Street**, the proto-hippies even established a free shop; no money changed hands but customers took what they wanted and left what they could.

As word of the goings-on in Haight-Ashbury spread in time across the city, there followed lurid newspaper exposés, predictably focusing on **sex and drugs**, that were soon taken up by the national media. Although intended to shock and outrage, for many disaffected young people in the troubled USA of the 1960s, the reportage of Haight-Ashbury had precisely the opposite effect: they packed their bags and promptly made their way west.

Above: *A wonderful example of the Stick style of Victorian house design.*
Left: *Sandals are almost* de rigeur *on laid-back Haight Street.*
Opposite: *Junction of Haight and Ashbury.*

HAIGHT AND ASHBURY

The streets of Haight and Ashbury were named after two important figures in 19th-century San Francisco. **Henry H Haight**, a lawyer, arrived in the throes of the Gold Rush in 1850. Entering politics, he became the state of California's tenth governor. Though generally regarded as a fair man of high moral principles, Haight advocated an end to Chinese immigration and opposed suffrage for blacks. **Monroe Ashbury** was a member of the city's Board of Supervisors active in the city's 1860s westward expansion into the Outside Lands.

Hippie Chronicles

Much has been written about Haight-Ashbury in the 1960s but there are two books which come closer than most to telling the true story. **Ralph J Gleason** was a generation older than the first hippies but as a music journalist with the *San Francisco Chronicle* covered many of the early events. With the almost contemporaneous (published 1969) *The Jefferson Airplane and the San Francisco Sound*, Gleason captures interviews with the best-known musicians. A more sober, hindsight view is provided by Charles Perry's *The Haight-Ashbury: A History*, a detailed account of the era, written in the 1980s.

Haight-Ashbury today is not only laden with landmarks of the hippie era but still has a strong sense of the unconventional, with punks riding skateboards, grunge musicians busking on the streets, a plethora of record and book shops, and some of the city's best vintage-clothing outlets – there is probably no better place in the world to buy tie-dyed T-shirts. For the first time since its creation, Haight-Ashbury is also in the throes of upward mobility, with a growing band of expensive restaurants and designer clothing stores, and ever-rising rents in its hundreds of now carefully restored and preserved Victorian houses.

Below: *Haight-Ashbury is generously endowed with fine architecture.*

Hippie landmarks

Anyone drawn to Haight-Ashbury for its hippie associations will find plenty to please on even the shortest stroll through the neighbourhood. Inextricably linked to Haight-Ashbury psychedelia, the long-running rock group the Grateful Dead (formed in 1964 as the Warlocks and finally splitting up in 1995) played free concerts and encouraged community activities from various local addresses. But the group is most famously linked with the pretty Queen-Anne house at **710 Ashbury Street**, which the band members occupied from 1966.

The other stalwarts of the local psychedelic scene were the Jefferson Airplane, who occupied an expansive home at **2400 Fulton Street**, facing Golden Gate Park. Among other Haight-Ashbury residents was singer Janis Joplin, who came from Texas but whose career took off while she lived at **112 Lyon Street**.

Perhaps one of the most lastingly beneficial developments of the Summer of Love was the creation of the Haight-Ashbury Free Clinic, at the junction of Clayton and Haight streets. Founded by an idealistic young doctor, the clinic provided free health care to hippies, who were otherwise ignored by the city's medical institutions. The hippies may have largely gone but the free clinic continues to serve the poor, not only in Haight-Ashbury but from other sites across the Bay Area.

Above: *Pipe Dreams, selling accessories for the serious smoker.*

The Grateful Dead, Jefferson Airplane and Jimi Hendrix were among the rock music icons of the 1960s who appeared at the **Straight Theater**, 1660 Haight Street, now a vintage clothing store. In a law-bending stunt typical of the times, the venue's promoters had no license to stage live music but claimed instead that they were running a dance school.

A block north of Haight Street, the **Panhandle** is a slender eight-block-long wedge of greenery laid out in the late-19th century as an adjunct to Golden Gate Park. Initially a private park and still lined by the elegant Victorian homes contemporaneous with its creation, the Panhandle was far from private during the 1960s when it provided a forum for numerous free concerts.

A less fondly remembered landmark is the former residence of **Charles Manson**, who lived with his followers at 636 Cole Street before moving to southern California and becoming involved in a series of infamously grisly murders.

A Haight-Ashbury Walking Tour

There are many guided walking tours in San Francisco but only the **Flower Power Tour** concentrates exclusively on Haight-Ashbury, providing endless anecdotes about the psychedelic 1960s as well as outlining the development of the neighbourhood and pausing outside some of its most impressive Victorian architecture. The walk takes place at least twice weekly according to demand and lasts 2 hours. For reservations, tel: (415) 836–1621.

MASONIC AVENUE ARCHITECTURE

Alamo Square and **Buena Vista Park** hold some of Haight-Ashbury's most notable old homes but many more view-worthy examples occur elsewhere around the neighbourhood. Masonic Avenue is one street that holds more than its share. On Masonic, look for the Bernard Maybeck-designed shingled home at number 1526; the Queen Anne style home with modern stained glass windows at 1450; and the row of dwellings in the vertically accented Stick style at numbers 1322–1342.

Buena Vista Park **

With 36 acres (14.4ha) of jungle-like entwinements consisting of tree roots and branches, the reward for scrambling up the overgrown pathway to the top of **Buena Vista Park**, just off Haight Street, is a fine view across the city and a considerable feeling of achievement. Easier to complete is a walk along **Buena Vista Avenue**, lined by appealing Victorian homes. Foremost among them is the **Spreckels Mansion**, 737 Buena Vista Avenue, which was completed in 1898 for Richard Spreckels. Now once again a private residence, the mansion served for a time as a boarding house and, in the 1960s, as a recording studio used by the Grateful Dead and others.

Alamo Square **

One of the most commonly reproduced images of San Francisco depicts the Financial District's modern skyscrapers rising in the distance behind six brightly painted Victorian houses on Alamo Square. The houses, erected in the 1890s, are on the east side of the square; the centre is occupied by a sloping, tree-lined park. Many equally attractive and photogenic late-19th-century homes line the square, including the **Westerfield House**, on the north side at 1189 Fulton Street, an impressive example of the vertically accented Stick style.

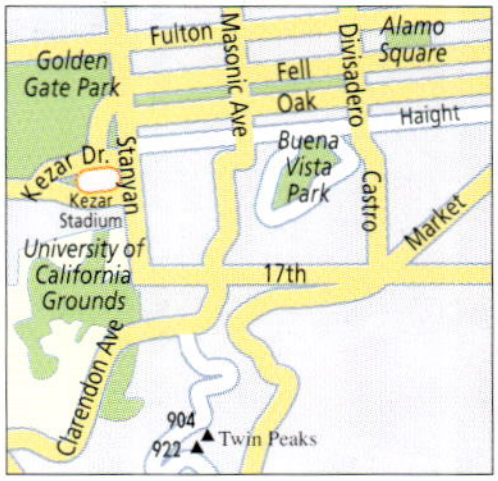

Lower Haight *

Returning to Haight Street from Alamo Square and continuing east leads into the area known as Lower Haight. The rising rents of Haight-Ashbury have helped this become the current neighbourhood of choice for many artists, musicians and unconventional creative types who live in these spacious but affordable houses. The offbeat cafés, shops and galleries found along the 500 block of Haight Street capture the spirit of the area.

Opposite: *The east side of Alamo Square with the Financial District in the background, probably the most photographed view in San Francisco.*

The Church of John Coltrane *

Seeing the celebrated jazz saxophonist John Coltrane play live in the 1960s and subsequently learning of Coltrane's belief in God, inspired one San Francisco jazz fan to embark on the road that would make him a bishop and the leader of the congregation that gathers for Sunday service at St John's African Orthodox Church, 930 Gough Street, known as the Church of John Coltrane. The four-hour service finds the bishop blowing a sax and members of the congregation playing instruments of their own.

Twin Peaks

Rising just over 900ft (274m) to the south of Haight-Ashbury, the two hills known as Twin Peaks provide one of the best vantage points for gazing across the city and parts of the Bay Area. Zig-zagging residential streets lie at the foot of the slopes and a twisting road leads up to a lookout point. Spanish settlers in San Francisco had a different name for the hills, calling them *Los Pechos de la Chola*, or 'Breasts of the Indian Girl'.

Literary Haight-Ashbury

Though they play second fiddle to the psychedelic hotspots, Haight-Ashbury holds its share of literary landmarks. The popular 1920s novelist **Kathleen Thompson** found acclaim in New York but retained her spacious home at 1901 Page Street. Author of *The Human Comedy* and a Pulitzer-prize winning play, **William Sayoran** was first published while living at 348 Carl Street in the 1930s. Also successful during the 1930s was **Kay Boyle**, who lived at 419 Frederick Street while teaching at San Francisco State University. More in keeping with the area's anarchic spirit, **Hunter S Thompson** perfected his rabid gonzo journalism style while living at 318 Parnassus Avenue and writing *Hells Angels*.

The Japanese Tea Garden

Even if you come to Golden Gate Park chiefly for its museums, do not miss the nearby **Japanese Tea Garden**. With footpaths weaving around blazing flower beds, bonsai trees and carp-filled ponds, the compact garden is a delight. In the garden's heart is a bronze Buddha, cast in Japan and dating from 1790. Laid out at the time of the 1894 Midwinter International Exposition, the garden was tended for many years by **Makota Hagiwara**, a Japanese San Franciscan credited with inventing the fortune cookie as a treat for garden visitors; the idea was later adopted by Chinatown restaurants.

Golden Gate Park

A verdant rectangular slab between Haight-Ashbury and the Pacific Ocean, Golden Gate Park fills 1017 acres (412ha), space enough for a golf course, a polo field, a herd of buffalo, riding stables, windmills, several lakes, and two of San Francisco's most popular visitor attractions: the M H de Young Museum and the California Academy of Sciences. Because of the extra space created by the relocation of the Asian Art Museum to Civic Center, the MH de Young Museum closed for several years to rearrange its galleries and is due to re-open in 2005.

The park was miraculously cultivated in the late 1800s from an area of sand dunes then some distance from the general sway of San Francisco life. Much of the credit for creating what is now among the world's finest urban parks is due to the Scots-born **John McLaren**. One of the most individualistic figures in San Francisco's history, McLaren, who arrived in California in 1864, was appointed city parks supervisor in 1890 and continued shaping Golden Gate Park until his death in 1943; the city passed a special law enabling him to work beyond retirement age. MacLaren's vision was a park without buildings or statuary, and one where nature, with some subtle human directing, could largely run its course. Despite this, business interests led to the park's first building – erected for the 1894 Mid-winter International Exposition, intended to convince potential investors that San Francisco had a

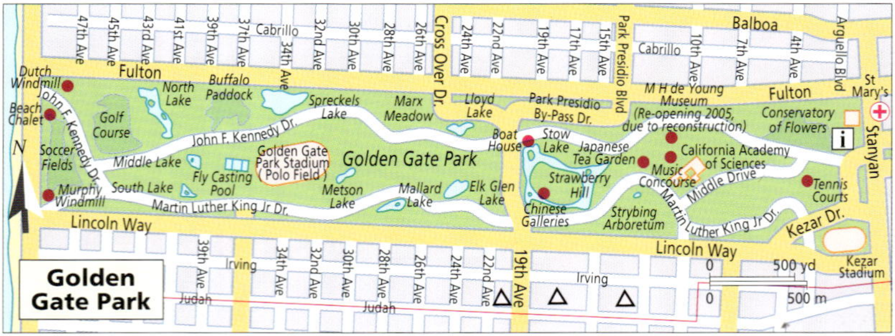

Above: *Carefully nurtured flower beds flank the steps that lead to the Conservatory of Flowers in Golden Gate Park.*

Mediterranean climate – and a rash of statuary followed. The Exposition was the first event to use the park as a symbol and showpiece of the city, a role it still fulfils with great style, despite the compromising of McLaren's vision.

Only the keenest walkers sensibly attempt to cover all the amply-proportioned park by foot. A better bet is to hire a bike from the outlets along Stanyan Street facing the eastern edge, or to focus on a small section of the parks nooks and crannies.

A fitting first stop might be the **John McLaren Rhododendron Dell** where a modest statue depicts the parks creator surrounded by his favourite plants, rhododendrons, while gazing intently at a pine cone. Nearby among the park's many secluded groves is the 15-acre **Aids Memorial Grove**, scene of many Aids-related funerals and intended as a fitting place to remember loved ones lost to the disease.

The M H de Young Museum (re-opening in 2005) and the California Academy of Sciences (see below) stand close to the **Music Concourse**, created for the 1894 Mid-Winter Fair. Beyond it to the south, the **Strybing Arboretum and Botanical Gardens** hold 6000 plant species across 70 bucolic acres, which include the **Redwood Trail**, a footpath winding around some diminutive examples of California's redwood trees.

The Conservatory of Flowers

Elegant floral gardens surrounded by groves of camellias, fuchsias and dahlias, and overlooked by palm trees, make the approach to Golden Gate Park's **Conservatory of Flowers** a dazzling one. Commissioned from an Irish company by prominent California landowner James Lick in 1875, the conservatory was assembled here in 1879 after being shipped around Cape Horn. Now the oldest building in the park, the conservatory's steamy interior holds a vibrant display of tropical flora and a tremendous collection of orchids.

Further west, Stow Lake is a reservoir assisting the park's irrigation and is dominated by **Strawberry Hill**, rising to 130m (428ft) high in its centre. If a boat glide aroung the lake (hire one from the lakeside boathouse) seems insufficiently strenuous, cross one of the two bridges and tackle a footpath to the hill's summit. The reward for doing so is a memorable view across the park.

Passing Cross Over Drive, a busy road which connects the Sunset and Richmond districts on either side of the park, leads you to the park's main recreational venues. These include an equestrian area, a dog-training field, four soccer fields, and **Spreckels Lake** which is given over to the voyages of radio-controlled model yachts and powerboats.

Also here is the **Polo Field** (formally titled Golden Gate Park Stadium) which, for many conversant with 1960s San Francisco, is less synonymous with polo than with the heyday of flower-power when it hosted rock concerts, communal LSD trips, and the legendary Human Be-In event of 1967. In keeping with the mood of the times, the Be-In began with a Hindu blessing of the space by the poets Allen Ginsberg and Gary Snyder, continued with orations from LSD guru Timothy Leary, music from the Grateful Dead and others, before being brought to an end with the blowing of a conch shell. As if to bring the 1960s to a belated conclusion, 200,000 people packed the Polo Field in November 1991 for a free concert marking

THE IMPOSSIBLE PARK

The area now consumed by Golden Gate Park was previously part of the 'Outside Lands', a barren expanse of sand dunes occupied by squatters. Claiming it under a law dating from the time of Mexican rule in California, the city acquired the land in 1870. Nonetheless, famed urban landscaper Frederick Law Olmsted, creator of New York's Central Park, looked at the desolate terrain and declared the creation of a park on top of it as 'impossible'.

the death of Bill Graham, a legendary rock music promoter closely linked with the decade.

On the park's western border, facing Great Highway and the Pacific Ocean, the 1920s **Beach Chalet** was designed by Willis Polk and now holds a park **visitor information centre**. Drop in to admire the 1930s Lucien Labaudt murals which show San Franciscans at leisure in locations around the city.

California Academy of Sciences **

While many of its happiest visitors are children, adults too will find plenty to amuse and educate themselves within the California Academy of Sciences (daily 9:00 or 10:00 to 17:00 or 18:00), where hands-on displays explore the fundamentals of the natural world (the adjoining Morrison Planetarium explores the realms beyond this) and alligators, penguins and dolphins feature among a wide variety of animal life.

North America's most diverse display of underwater life is found within the **Steinhart Aquarium**, while close at hand is the viewing gallery encircled by the 100,000-gallon (380,000 litre) tank of the remarkable **Fish Roundabout**, featuring fast-swimming denizens of the deep such as snappers, seabass and leopard sharks. A breeding colony of black-footed penguins also lives nearby, as do the creatures of the **California Tidepool** and **The Swamp**, where a waterfall trickles into dense subtropical foliage providing cover for lurking frogs, lizards, alligators and crocodiles.

Another excellent display among the science exhibits is the **Safequake**, which recreates the streets of San Francisco as they shook during the major earthquakes of 1865 and 1906.

PARK WINDMILLS

Two picturesque windmills stand at the western end of Golden Gate Park. Just off JF Kennedy Drive, the **Dutch Windmill** was erected in 1902 as part of a scheme to irrigate the park by pumping water from an underground river. In keeping with the Dutch theme, the windmill overlooks the Queen Wihelmina Tulip Garden, at its best during the springtime blooming season. The success of the Dutch windmill, able to pump 30,000 gallons (114,000 litres) of water an hour, led to a second windmill, the **Murphy Windmill**, being raised in 1905. Since the city authorities took charge of the water supply in 1929, both windmills have led entirely decorative lives.

Opposite: *The Pagoda of Golden Gate Park's delightful Japanese Garden is almost hidden by shrubbery.*

Left: *As well as windmills, museums, an aquarium, stables, buffalo and boating lakes, Golden Gate Park contains a host of statuary including this Cervantes Memorial.*

LIFEGUARD
OCEAN KAYAK

8
Northwest San Francisco

North of Golden Gate Park lie the broad streets and comfortable middle-class homes of the **Richmond District**. Much of the area seems more like a suburban town than a city neighbourhood but what it lacks in clear-cut visitor targets it compensates for with a curious ethnic mixture ranging from Chinese-Americans, wealthy enough for Chinatown to be a distant memory, to numerous eastern European groups who have settled here over the last 100 years, most obvious among them being the Russians with their imposing Orthodox cathedral.

Another bucolic area borders the Richmond District to the north but, unlike the predominantly flat Golden Gate Park, much of the **Presidio** is a hilly area with pockets of complete wildness. Until recently a military base, the Presidio's history – it was founded by the Spanish – is entertainingly detailed at a small museum while the surrounds provide plenty of scope for nature rambles.

Like the Presidio, **Lincoln Park** rises sheer above the waters of the Golden Gate and is known to golfing San Franciscans for its very windy 18 holes. Everyone else, though, knows Lincoln Park for the excellent horde of European art and the many Rodin sculptures displayed at the California Palace of Honor.

The undeveloped northwestern coast of San Francisco is traversed by a network of footpaths that form the **Coastal Trail** which provides pedestrian access to several slender beaches and charts a spectacular route around the edge of the city, high above the choppy waves of the Golden Gate and far from traffic and crowds.

Don't Miss

***** California Palace of the Legion of Honor Galleries:** packed with fabulous European art and a special stash of Rodin sculptures.
**** Coastal Trail:** brave the winds howling through the Golden Gate on this exhilarating route around the city's wild northwestern edge.
**** The Presidio:** one-time Spanish settlement and military base, with an excellent small museum and many miles of nature trails.

Opposite: *Venturing into the sea from Baker Beach, along the coastal trail.*

The Neptune Society Columbarium

One of the strangest sights in San Francisco is the Neptune Society Columbarium, at 1 Loraine Court in the Richmond District. Opened in 1898, the Columbarium stores the ashes of some 20,000 deceased San Franciscans in individual niches set into walls beneath an elegant rotunda. The building is open each morning with guided tours on Saturdays, pointing out some of the more entertainingly decorated niches; some have painted landscapes and one holds a miniature set of golf clubs.

Richmond District

Reflecting San Francisco's ethnically diverse make-up and the continually changing demographics of its neighbourhoods, the Richmond District was predominantly inhabited by East European immigrants, especially Russians, and their descendants until the 1970s when growing numbers of well-established **Chinese-American** families left the confines of Chinatown for a more comfortable life in the spacious homes that line the Richmond District's tidy streets.

The main commercial artery is **Clement Street**, along which are dozens of busy Chinese restaurants and bakeries, a smattering of general stores and a few very browsable, used-book shops.

Unlike the rural Russians – often dissenters from the Orthodox religion and members of pietistic sects – who settled in the south of the city during the 1850s, the

Richmond District **Russians** were typically a more aristocratic breed, many of them military officers who arrived on the heels of the Bolshevik revolution. Some 25,000 Russian-Americans still live in and around the Richmond District. The most striking reminder of their presence is the **Holy Virgin Cathedral**, 6210 Geary Boulevard. Resplendent with golden onion domes, it was opened in 1961.

Significant numbers among the district's influx of Russians and East Europeans were Jewish. On the northern fringe of the area rises the striking, red-tiled, Byzantine-style dome of **Temple Emanu-El**, at the junction of Lake Street and Arguello Boulevard. The 2000-seat synagogue, which was completed in 1926 for $3 million, is open for short guided tours (Monday-Friday 13:00–15:00).

THE PRESIDIO'S DOOMED ROMANCE

In 1806, the commandant of the Spanish *presidio* received an unexpected visitor in the form of **Nikolai Rezanov**, leader of an expedition to California on behalf of the Russian-American Fur Company. Initially suspicious, the commandant warmed to Rezanov, as did his teenage daughter, **Doña Concepción**, to whom Rezanov became engaged. Seeking Tsarist and papal approval of the marriage, Rezanov left for St Petersburg but died in Siberia after falling from his horse. Allegedly, Doña Concepción waited patiently for Rezanov's return, spurning other offers of marriage and only learning of his death 36 years later.

THE PRESIDIO

Rare is the city able to keep a massive chunk of itself in a wild and bucolic state, but San Francisco succeeds with the 1480 acres (599ha) of hills, woods, grassy marshlands and sandy beaches that form the Presidio, covering its northwest corner and overlooking the Golden Gate.

The reason for the area's lack of development is a military one. Until being decommissioned in 1994, the Presidio served as the headquarters of the US Sixth Army although its role as an armed forces base stretches back to San Francisco's earliest days. In 1776, the **Spanish** founded a *presidio*, or garrison, here to deter incursion by rival colonial powers into the Golden Gate and to protect the new Mission Dolores.

As it turned out, the Presidio made a comfortable posting for numerous generations of US service personnel. The army was responsible for the thick groves of cypress, pine and eucalyptus trees that were planted in the 1880s to enhance the

Below: *Many people of Russian descent live in the Richmond District.*

base. The public have long enjoyed more or less free access to the area's network of walking, hiking and cycling trails, and some San Franciscans have buried their deceased domestic animals in the pet cemetery. The Presidio is now under federal protection as part of the Golden Gate National Recreation Area (*see* p. 94).

Housed in a wooden building that served as a military hospital from 1864, the **Presidio Museum**, at the junction of Lincoln and Funston streets (Wednesday-Sunday 10:00–16:00), provides an excellent outline of the origins of the Presidio with maps and historical memorabilia, and does much to explain San Francisco's evolution. Numerous display cases of military uniforms, insignia and weaponry complement the story, but pride of place goes to a tremendous documentation of the earthquake and fire that decimated the city in 1906. The disaster rendered many San Franciscans homeless and a large number were temporarily housed in the cramped **'refugee cottages'**, examples of which can be seen to the rear of the building.

The buildings of the Presidio encompass many architectural styles but of particular note is the **Officers' Club**, 50 Moraga Avenue. Built in the 1930s in the Mission style, which was popular in California at the time, the club incorporates a few of the adobe bricks that remain from one of the oldest structures in the city, built here by the Spanish in the early 1800s.

The Presidio's sombre **National Military Cemetery** on Lincoln Boulevard is the final resting place of some 15,000 Americans, who perished in combat during the Civil War and thereafter. Generally more entertaining are the tombs and inscriptions of the nearby **Pets Cemetery**, originally intended for deceased army guard dogs but used by the general public since 1945.

Golden Gate National Recreation Area

In 1972, some privately owned land and former military areas, together with various city parks, were combined to became the federal-administered Golden Gate National Recreation Area (GGNRA). Since losing its army role the Presidio has been absorbed into the GGNRA, which now accounts for some 75,000 acres (30,353ha) of coastal San Francisco, from Fort Funston in the south to the Marin Headlands on the northern side of the Golden Gate. Much of the land is maintained in near-pristine state and is criss-crossed with hiking and cycling trails.

Below: *Diverse architecture in a neighbourhood street close to the Presidio.*

Above: *The approach to the California Palace of the Legion of Honor.*

Lincoln Park and the Coastal Trail

California Palace of the Legion of Honor ***

On a dramatic site above the Golden Gate, the **California Palace of the Legion of Honor**, Lincoln Park (Tuesday–Sunday 9:00–17:00), houses San Francisco's major trove of European art from 2500BC to the present century.

The collections stemmed from the friendship of Alma Spreckels, wife of wealthy San Franciscan Adolph Spreckels, with sculptor Auguste Rodin, whom she first met in Paris. A further factor in the creation of the museum was the bitter rivalry between the Spreckels and another prominent San Francisco family, the newspaper-owning de Youngs. When the M H De Young Museum of Art opened in Golden Gate Park, the Spreckel's were determined not to be outdone and to make their own name equally synonymous with publicly accessible artworks. The California Palace of the Legion of Honor opened on Armistice Day 1924, and was dedicated to California's dead of World War I.

In the early 1990s the museum underwent a $34.6 million restructuring in order to meet new earthquake safety standards and, at the same time, creating a series of beautifully lit and sympathetically designed galleries.

Alma Spreckels

Studying at the forerunner of the San Francisco Art Institute, San Francisco-born **Alma de Bretteville** was selected by her tutor as a model for the figure of *Victory* that tops the Dewey Monument in Union Square. She found much greater fame, however, after marrying the 50-year-old rich sugar mogul **Adolph Spreckels**, 26 years her senior, in 1908. As well as founding the California Palace of the Legion of Honor, the couple had built the grand Spreckels Mansion in Pacific Heights (*see* p. 65). Following Adolph's death in 1924, Alma administered the family sugar business and remained a part of San Francisco's high society until her own death in 1968.

Alma Spreckels first met Rodin in 1914 and began collecting his work a year later by buying several pieces exhibited at San Francisco's Panama Pacific Exposition. Her Rodin collection grew steadily to around 70 items – many from the sculptor's own studio – and has been greatly expanded since her death. Outside the main entrance to the museum stands a *Thinker* from the original cast and inside, in the Rodin Room, are selections from some 400 Rodin pieces spanning most of his career, including one of his most important early works, *Man With A Broken Nose*.

Drawn from many eras, the **European paintings** are an inevitably mixed batch. Highlights include the Dutch and Flemish collections where Rubens' *The Tribute Money* stands out. Painted in around 1612, the work bears the influence of the artist's time spent in Italy. Another major offering is El Greco's *Saint John the Baptist*, the landscape and sky behind the elongated body of John seemingly charged by his spiritual energy. Comparatively recent pieces to watch for are Seurat's *Eiffel Tower*, a shimmering depiction of the eponymous tower in the artist's noted pointillist style, and Edward Degas's amusing *The Impressario*.

With some 100,000 works on paper, the **Achenbach Foundation for Graphic Arts** is the largest repository of its kind in the western USA. Selections from the collection, often augmented with loans, form special exhibitions of great quality that are shown on the museum's lower level.

A sombre reminder of Nazi atrocities, George Segal's *Holocaust* sculpture is among the museum's most powerful pieces but is often missed by visitors as it is situated along a short path that leads from the car park.

Lincoln Park's Past

In 1860, when what is now Lincoln Park still stood outside the boundaries of San Francisco and mostly comprised scrubland, around 200 acres (80ha) were selected by the authorities for a pauper's burial ground known as **Golden Gate Cemetery**. As San Francisco expanded, pressure increased for burials to be barred from the city and, in 1901, city cemeteries were closed and many of the dead were moved to Colma, just south of the city. Nonetheless, many thousands of bodies are believed to have remained at Golden Gate Cemetery and now lie under the Lincoln Park golf course.

The Coastal Trail **

Besides making a scenically splendid setting for the California Palace of the Legion of Honor, Lincoln Park boasts one of the world's most spectacularly situated public golf courses. Anyone tackling these blustery 18 holes is treated to vistas of the Golden Gate with Marin County's stark, dramatic headlands as a backdrop.

Lincoln Park rises sheer above the Golden Gate and is linked by steep footpaths to the **coastal trail**, an enjoyable, if windswept, route around the city's northwestern corner. Running more or less between the Golden Gate Bridge and the Cliff House and threading its way through sometimes dense vegetation and along tall cliffs, the trail – part of the Golden Gate National Recreation Area (*see* p. 94) – also links several slender beaches. Wend your way down to any of these sandy stretches and the bustling city suddenly seems very far away.

The longest of these beaches, the mile-long **Baker Beach**, is unsafe for swimming but much appreciated by local anglers and in-the-know beachcombers and sunbathers. At weekends, a park ranger is on hand to deliver a talk about **Battery Chamberlin**, the beach's war-time fortification, and to demonstrate the workings of a 95,000-pound (43,084kg) cannon, a replica of one which stood here from 1904 awaiting enemy incursions into the Golden Gate.

Opposite: *Seurat's painting of the Eiffel Tower, a marvel of engineering like the Golden Gate Bridge, is on display in the California Palace of the Legion of Honour.*
Below: *Dressed for the chilly winds that whip ashore off the Golden Gate, locals stroll down Baker Beach.*

Above: *Sea lions inhabit Seal Rock, close to the Cliff House.*

Ocean Beach and the Great Highway

The view looking south from Sutro Heights Park and the Cliff House is an inviting one, taking in – fogs permitting – a sizeable chunk of the city's Pacific Coast and the 4-mile (6.4km) Ocean Beach. Though the waters are too cold and too afflicted by undertow to allow safe swimming, the beach is a popular place to jog, walk dogs and fly kites, and has been designated public land since 1868. Bordering the beach for its entire length, Great Highway was first laid out in 1873.

Immediately west of Baker Beach the coastal trail is interrupted by the wealthy residential area of **Seacliff**, the well-tended streets of which provide access to secluded China Beach. Walled by steep cliffs and named after the Chinese fishermen who lived in shacks here during the Gold Rush, the beach is one of only a handful in San Francisco where swimming is permitted (May to October only), although the waters are never warm.

West of Seacliff the coastal trail picks over steep hills from where there are vertiginous views of the Golden Gate. Divergent paths, that need to be approached with caution as this section of the route is liable to be flooded by rising tides, lead down to **Land's End**, a pocket-sized beach enclosed by cypress and pine trees where swimming is not allowed.

The western limit of the coastal trail is close to the **Sutro Bath ruins**. The crumbling stonework remains do little to suggest the former glory of the baths, which were enormously popular with San Franciscans from the 1890s to the 1920s. Devised with an ingenious pumping system, the baths covered a 3-acre (1.2ha) plot where people could swim indoors in heated ocean water and participate in numerous special events for a token fee.

The baths were the creation of **Adolph Sutro**, an extremely wealthy and altruistic one-time city mayor who made his fortune from silver mines, as well as from his invention of a ventilation system for mine tunnels. Sutro died in 1898 and following his death the baths declined in popularity.

Unfortunately, structural repairs were neglected and the baths gradually crumbled. They were finally destroyed by fire in 1966.

Across Point Lobos Avenue from the ruins, **Sutro Heights Park** is an invitingly green open space that once formed part of the grounds of Adolph Sutro's mansion, built here in the 1880s. Although little remains from Sutro's time, with the exception of a few sculptured lions and flower beds, the park offers wonderful views across Golden Gate Park and along San Francisco's dramatic coastline.

USS San Francisco Memorial

Launched in 1933, the cruiser *USS San Francisco* was the second ship to bear the name of the city and the first war ship to be launched during the presidency of Franklin Roosevelt. The *San Francisco* was docked in Pearl Harbour when the Japanese attacked in December 1941, bringing the USA into World War II. The ship went on to see action throughout the Pacific before being decommissioned in 1946. Overlooking Land's End, the *USS San Francisco* memorial comprises part of the ship's bridge (with shell damage visible) and mast.

The Cliff House *

Perched on a cliff top opposite Sutro Heights Park, the present **Cliff House** is the latest of several structures to occupy the site since 1863. In its original incarnation, the Cliff House was a celebrated meeting place for the rich and famous. The third Cliff House, raised by Adolph Sutro in 1898, was an extraordinarily ornate eight-storey creation that loosely resembled a French chateau and which nowadays often features in photographic collections of bygone San Francisco.

Unlike its forbears, the current Cliff House is of little architectural merit but provides a good place from which to observe the **sea lions** on the inappropriately named Seal Rock, a series of rocky outcrops a short distance offshore. To the rear of the Cliff House restaurant is a **Visitor Information Centre** that dispenses general tips, maps and leaflets on San Francisco and the Golden Gate National Recreation Area.

Adolph Sutro: The Unhappy Mayor

Adolph Sutro's business battles with the **Big Four**, the widely despised millionaire railroad barons and land owners who dominated California life in the late 1800s, brought him considerable respect among the ordinary people of the city. In 1894, agreeing to stand only in the belief he would not win, Sutro was elected San Francisco's mayor. Though pledged to a popular anti-corruption programme, Sutro hated having to grapple with the machinations of City Hall and described the end of his two-year term as a 'perfect blessing'.

9
Touring the Bay Area

San Francisco is but one aspect of the Bay Area, which describes the communities on the north and east sides of San Francisco Bay whose fortunes are closely linked to that of the city, yet each retain a distinct character.

Berkeley is best known for its university campus, which provided the impetus for student uprisings across the nation in the 1960s and still dominates the entire community. With revolution no longer brewing on campus, attention should instead be focused on Berkeley's several fine museums and a number of architecturally impressive buildings dating back to the university's early days.

Oakland, immediately south of Berkeley, has none of the intellectual heritage of its neighbour but does have several districts well worth exploring. Housing a wonderful collection devoted entirely to the Golden State, the Oakland Museum of California is not to be missed.

A short ferry ride from the city lie **Sausalito** and **Tiburon**, two envy-inducing settlements inhabited by wealthy city commuters able to afford the rustic-looking, luxurious homes set into the steep hillsides. Besides a feast of souvenir shopping, Sausalito has an intriguing permanent exhibition, the Bay Model. In summer ferries continue from Tiburon to **Angel Island State Park**, an alluring tree-cloaked island with a hint of sadness in its past.

Across the Golden Gate Bridge the **Marin Headlands** provide a thrilling northern wall to the Golden Gate, the sense of untamed nature continuing to popular **Stinson Beach** and inland to **Muir Woods National Monument** with its splendid grove of redwood trees.

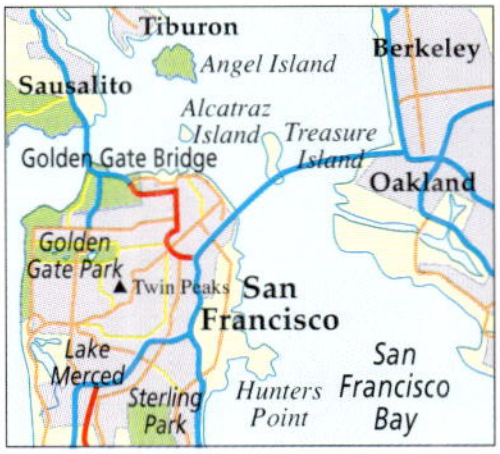

DON'T MISS

*** **Berkeley Campus:** seat of 1960's student radicalism; now notable for its museums and architectural landmarks.
*** **Oakland Museum of California:** a comprehensive and imaginatively presented insider's guide to California's past, present and future.
** **Sausalito:** a scenically perfect bayside community.
** **Marin Headlands:** forms the Golden Gate's rugged and blustery northern wall.
** **Muir Woods National Monument:** dark, damp woodlands, holding a much-visited grove of redwood trees.

Opposite: *The Bay Area is one of few places where the mighty redwood grows.*

Audubon Canyon Ranch
Alpine Lake
Mt Tamalpais
2571 ft
Bolinas Lagoon
Marin County
Stinson Beach
Muir Woods National Monument
Mill Valley
Greenbrae
Richmond San Rafael Bridge
Richmond
Contra Costa County
Strawberry Point
Tiburon
Bay Model
Richardson Bay
Angel Island State Park
Angel Island
Muir Beach
Marin City
Marin Headlands
Sausalito
Berkeley
University of California at Berkeley
Rodeo Beach
Visitors Center
Lighthouse
Point Bonita
Alcatraz Island
Treasure Island
Golden Gate Bridge
Oakland
Oakland Museum of California
S.F. - Oakland Bay Bridge
US Naval Air Station
San Francisco
Golden Gate Park
Ocean Beach
Alameda
San Francisco County
Alameda County
Fort Funston
Lake Merced
Hunters Point
Oakland International Airport
Daly City
Sterling Park
Broadmoor
San Francisco Bay
PACIFIC OCEAN
South San Francisco
San Bruno
Pacifica
San Francisco International Airport
San Pedro Pt
Gray Whale Cove
San Andreas Lake
Burlingame
San Mateo Bridge
N
San Mateo
Foster City
Montara
Pilarcitos Lake
Moss Beach
Lower Crystal Springs Reservoir
Belmont
Pillar Point
El Granada
Half Moon Bay
Redwood City
0
5 miles
5 km
Upper Crystal Springs Reservoir
Hetch Hetchy Aqueduct
San Mateo County
Menlo Park
Woodside
San Francisco Bay Area
101
580
80
1
131
13
880
61
280
35
82
92
84

Berkeley

Berkeley is dominated by the 30,000 students of the **University of California at Berkeley** (UCB) and its 100-acre (41ha) campus, situated a few minutes' walk north of the town's BART (underground transit) station. The student Free Speech Movement, which began at UCB in 1964 to protest campus issues, later helped inspire the massive anti-Vietnam War protests seen across the USA and also led to Berkeley becoming perceived as a hotbed of radicalism. Through the 1960s, peaceful student protest escalated into violent confrontations between young people and local police. By 1969, the National Guard – under order from future president Ronald Reagan, then governor of California – occupied the campus for 17 days. While student unrest is largely a thing of the past, the city of Berkeley is run by what is widely regarded as the most left-wing administration in the USA.

The campus can be explored easily on foot but be sure to get a map from the **Visitors Centre**, at the junction of University Avenue and Oxford Street, without which the complex of buildings and pathways will be confusing. Touring the campus museums and assorted landmarks will happily fill several hours.

University of California: The Origins

Founded in Oakland in 1869, the University of California moved to **Berkeley** in 1873, taking over an ailing Christian college. The fledgling university was beset by financial problems until receiving substantial donations from wealthy Californians, including **Phoebe Apperson Hearst** whose funds made possible the current Berkeley campus. Reflecting the economy of California, the university initially specialized in mining, mineralogy and agriculture, but diversified as and when the state's economy did. Over the years, the university expanded well beyond Berkeley and now has a series of campuses spread across the state.

Campus museums and exhibits **

The 11 galleries of the architecturally innovative **University Art Museum** (open Wednesday-Sunday 11:00–17:00; Thursday 11:00–21:00) stage temporary exhibitions, often of considerable merit and drawn from around the world. The permanent collection has a relatively low profile but includes the bold, colourful canvases of Hans Hoffman, a German-born artist who taught at Berkeley in the early 1930s and whose works helped launch the museum.

Below: *The Sather Tower (also known as the Campanile) rises from the heart of Berkeley campus.*

Campus Guided Tours

A mixture of historical and architectural information about the campus, and a wealth of personal anecdotal insights into Berkeley undergraduate life, can be acquired by joining a student-led free guided tour. The tours depart on Monday, Wednesday and Friday at 10:00 and 13:00 from the Visitors Center, near the junction of Oxford Street and University Avenue.

The changing exhibits at the **Phoebe Hearst Museum of Anthropology** (Wednesday-Sunday 10:00–16:30) are culled from the horde gathered by the university's own expeditions, which began in 1899 and have left few parts of the ancient world untouched. The museum is named after Phoebe Hearst, a founder of the university (and mother of the publishing tycoon, William Randolph Hearst) whose considerable wealth financed the earliest expeditions.

A permanent display tells the story of **Ishi**, a Native American believed to be the last surviving member of the Yahi tribe who avoided all contact with non-natives until 1911, when he was found wandering in northern California. Ishi lived at the museum (then in a different location) until his death in 1916, providing researchers with immense knowledge of native life.

One reason Ishi's people and their culture were lost was the sudden white settlement of California encouraged by the discovery of mineral riches. On the ground floor of the **Hearst School of Mining** are photographs and

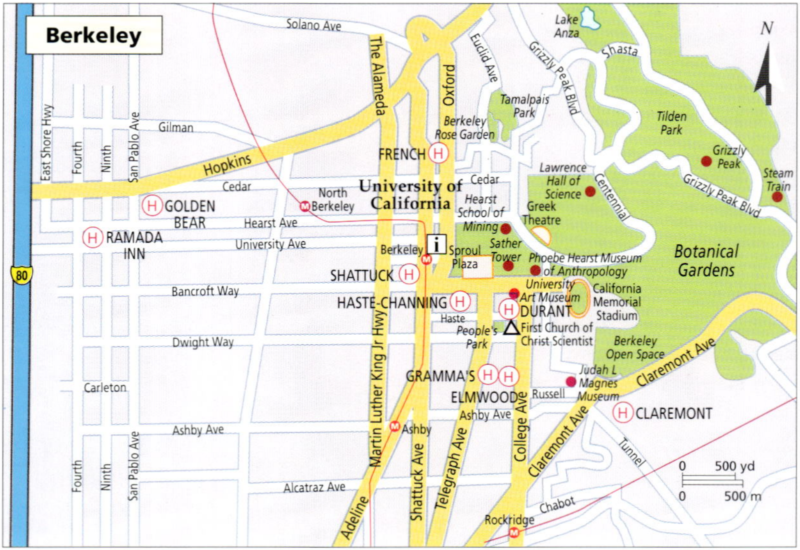

exhibits charting the rise of gold mining in California and the many underground treasures the state has yielded. To the rear of the building, an iron grill covers the entrance to the 200ft-deep (61m) practice mine, once used by students to develop their mining skills.

A display in the **Bancroft Library** of an 1849 gold nugget, surrounded by paintings of pioneer-era California and temporary exhibitions drawn from the library's 44 million books and manuscripts, also recalls California's early days.

Departing from the Hearst School of Mining, a bus winds into the hills that form the eastern section of the campus. Catching the bus avoids a leg-straining ascent to the **Lawrence Hall of Science** (daily 10:00–16:30) where the array of hands-on and interactive science exhibits fulfil a function similar to those at the Exploratorium (*see* p. 57). Outside the hall are fantastic views across Berkeley and over the bay to San Francisco.

Above: *Today's largely peaceful contingent of students at Berkeley pass through the Sather Gate on their way to and from lectures.*

Campus buildings and landmarks

Massachusetts-born architect **John Galen Howard** arrived in Berkeley in 1901 to oversee the construction of the university, and bestowed on the campus several of its most notable features. These include the **Sather Gate**, originally the main entrance to the campus and facing Telegraph Avenue, and the distinctive **Sather Tower** (commonly called 'the Campanile'), which was modelled on the belltower of St Mark's in Venice and rises to 307ft (94m) in the centre of the campus. Howard's celebrated beaux-arts influences are shown to great effect in the elegantly detailed **Hearst School of Mining**; completed in 1907, it is one of the campus's earliest buildings.

Confirming the immense popularity of Berkeley's sports teams is the 73,000-seat **California Memorial**

The Pacific Film Archive

The lower level of the University Art Museum holds the Pacific Film Archive, with a collection of some 6000 films spanning everything from renowned celluloid classics to arthouse cult movies. For film buffs, the daily screenings provide a welcome outlet for seldom-seen movies and works by against-the-grain directors. To find out what is playing today or forthcoming screenings, contact tel: (510) 642-1124; the number provides recorded information.

SCIENTIFIC BERKELEY

UCB has long been at the forefront of scientific research and attracts many of the US's finest brains. The world's first **cyclotron** (a type of particle accelerator) was built here in 1929 and a few years later **Robert Oppenheimer** joined the teaching faculty before being seconded to Los Alamos to oversee the creation of the first atomic bomb. Most research is conducted in the hills above the main campus where the **Lawrence Berkeley Laboratory** can be seen as part of a two-hour free tour, starting on Mondays from 10:00. Reservations are essential and must be made a week in advance, tel: (510) 486-5122.

Stadium, a showpiece venue completed in 1923. Any cracks that might be spotted in the terracing are likely to be caused by the movement of the Hayward Fault, which runs directly beneath the stadium and is one of hundreds of geological fault lines in the Bay Area.

The most relaxing place on campus is the **Morrison Library**, where deep armchairs and settees are arranged around tables laden with newspapers and magazines and shelves of general interest books, all intended for leisurely browsing.

Off Campus

Adjacent to the university, **Telegraph Avenue** comprises a lively collection of cafés, affordable ethnic eateries and well-stocked used-book stores. Within easy walking distance are **Peoples Park** (*see* p. 18), east between Haste Street and Dwight Way, and the architecturally extraordinary **First Church of Christ Scientist**, west at the junction of Dana Street and Dwight Way, created by the celebrated **Bernard Maybeck** (*see* p. 56) in 1910.

North of the campus lies Berkeley's so-called **Gourmet Ghetto**, a gathering of fashionable cafés and restaurants around the junction of Shattuck Avenue and Vine Street. Located at number 1517 is **Chez Panisse**, regarded as the establishment where, in the 1970s, the chef created what the rest of the culinary literate world came to know as 'California Cuisine', an imaginative mixture of French-influenced cooking combined with the best of the state's abundant natural produce and the cook's highly charged imagination.

GERTRUDE STEIN'S OAKLAND

Many have taken Gertrude Stein's comment on Oakland that 'there is no there, there' to be a stinging rebuke to the city she arrived in as a child in 1880 before spending much of her adult life in Paris. Such an interpretation is to take the quote, which appears in Stein's 1937 *Everybody's Autobiography*, out of context. Stein was in fact simply describing her slightly nostalgic reaction to the changes she found in Oakland when she visited during a lecture tour across the USA.

Oakland

Oakland may lack the allure of San Francisco and the academic renown of Berkeley, but this largely blue-collar city is an ethnically varied, mixed-income community with spacious parks, an immense lake and a successful redevelopment of both its waterfront and its downtown commercial area.

The complex of shops and restaurants on and around **Jack London Square** provide a first taste of Oakland for visitors arriving by ferry from San Francisco. Named after the writer who spent much of his childhood here and later worked in the Oakland docks, Jack London Square is also the site of **Heinhold's First and Last Chance Saloon** (a tiny bar in which London periodically drank) and the sod-covered log cabin claimed to be the one used by the writer during the 1897 Klondike gold rush in Alaska. A short walk north, Oakland's **Chinatown** is much less crowded than its San Francisco counterpart but is equally worth a visit – if only for its glut of dependable restaurants.

Opposite: *Berkeley's parks include the splendid Rose Garden, home to some 250 varieties of rose.*

Further north lies **Lake Merritt**, the world's largest saltwater lagoon and a scenic venue for watersports. Standing on the lake's edge, the restored 1876 **Camron Stanford House** (open Wednesday 11:00–16:00, and Sunday 13:00–17:00), 1418 Lakeside Drive, provides a peek into early Oakland life.

An excellent introductory film offers a fuller background on the growth of Oakland, a community long tired of having to play second-fiddle to that of San Francisco.

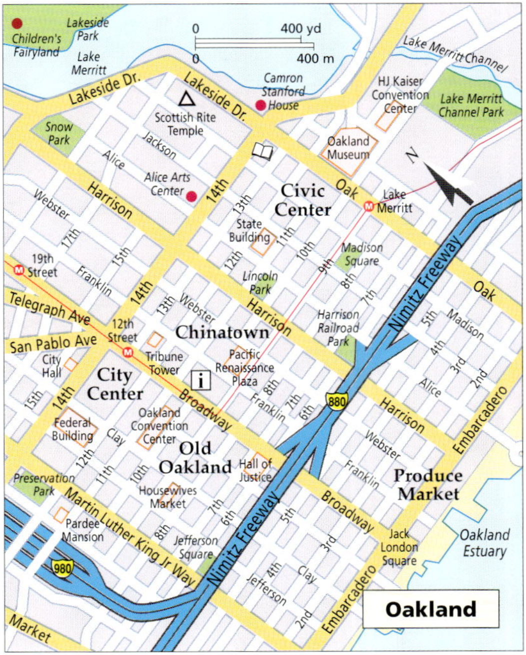

MUSEUM BACKGROUND

The only museum exclusively documenting the Golden State, the Oakland Museum of California grew from the amalgamation of three earlier museums, the Oakland Public Museum, the Oakland Art Museum and the Snow Museum of Natural History, and opened in 1969. The museum occupies one of the Bay Area's most critically acclaimed buildings, the cleverly designed multi-leveled structure making possible the interior's spacious galleries and the well-tended terraced gardens that spread around the exterior and continue on to the building's roof.

Above: *A prominent 1930s movie theater near the centre of Oakland.*

SAUSALITO AND WHALING

Sausalito was a major whaling port for much of the 19th century. Attracted by the proximity to the Arctic Ocean, with its stocks of gray and humpback whales, and the ready market for whale products provided by California, whaling vessels arrived from far and wide, including the major US whaling centres of New England. The invention of kerosene in the 1850s lessened the demand for whale oil, although the mammals continued to be hunted off California into the early 1900s for whale bone, a major component of ladies corsets.

Oakland Museum of California ***

However enjoyable the rest of Oakland may be, the main justification for a visit is to tour the tremendous collection of California art, history, and natural history that fills the three floors of the **Oakland Museum of California**, 1000 Oak Street (Wednesday-Saturday 10:00-17:00, Sunday 12:00-19:00).

At ground level, the **Hall of Ecology** and **Aquatic California Gallery** examines the diversity of natural California, from the birdlife of the deserts to the marine life of the oceans with texts and dioramas.

The second floor **Cowell Hall of History** deals with the human story of California. The displays begin with the many native groups who inhabited the region prior to European arrival and progress as far as examining the global impact of personal computers, invented in Silicon Valley – the popular name for the high-tech industrial area around San Jose, south of San Francisco. Amid pioneer-period wagons and 1950s souvenirs of Disneyland, the exhibits are numerous and accessibly arranged. There are no descriptive texts for individual items and visitors are encouraged to make use of friendly computers to find out more; the easy-to-use terminals also offer the opportunity to explore particular historical avenues more thoroughly.

On the top floor, the collection of Californian art is arranged to show the swift progress of the state's artistic achievements, from rough sketches of Gold-Rush scenes to the multi-media work of contemporary artists.

Marin County

Sausalito **

It has been a smugglers' lair, a fishing village, a whaling port and the site of a large shipyard but today Sausalito is a well-to-do suburb of San Francisco with pretensions to being a Mediterranean-style artists' colony.

Spread around the edge of the bay and quickly climbing into a tree-cloaked hillside, Sausalito has a gorgeous location. The views toward San Francisco are memorable and there is much to be enjoyed by simply striding up and down steep streets admiring the many picturesque and expensive homes.

Sausalito is a very popular destination and is usually besieged by day-trippers. To avoid the crowds, it is a wise move to arrive on a relatively early (any time before 11:00) midweek ferry. One of the few Sausalito streets that does not need to be climbed is **Bridgeway**, the community's sea-level, main thoroughfare. Roughly 1¼ miles (2km) along Bridgeway from the ferry dock lies the excellent **Bay Model**, 2100 Bridgeway (Tuesday-Friday 09:00–16:00;

Below: *The well-to-do homes of Sausalito climb the tree-covered hillside at the northeastern end of San Francisco Bay.*

WILLIAM RICHARDSON

English-born William Richardson landed in San Francisco Bay as first mate on a whaling ship in 1822. Adopting the Catholic faith, Richardson curried favour with the commandant of the Spanish *presidio* and married his daughter. Richardson built the first home in what became Yerba Buena (the early name of San Francisco) and in 1838 acquired a 20,000-acre (8094ha) land grant on what the Spanish had named *saucelito* ('willow grove'), today's Sausalito. Richardson's responsibilities included enforcing the Mexican trade ban on US ships and collecting ship's taxes. Allegedly, he also masterminded smuggling operations; one of Sausalito's sheltered bays is still known as Smuggler's Cove.

weekends 09:00–18:00). Built by the US Army Corps of Engineers, the model is the size of an American football pitch and produces an accurate replication of the tides and currents of San Francisco Bay. A short film describes the purpose and the workings of the model, and marked walkways lead into and around the model itself, the route interspersed with texts and displays on various aspects of the bay's ecology.

Tiburon *

Enjoying a similarly appealing setting beside the bay, Tiburon is slightly less busy than Sausalito and its speciality shops, though aimed at day-trippers, generally have a homelier atmosphere and are more enjoyable to browse. Many of the shops along Main Street are brightly painted, and some – making up the area known as **Ark Row** – are actually 19th-century houseboats which have been pulled permanently ashore.

Angel Island State Park **

The largest island in San Francisco Bay, Angel Island State Park is ideal for hiking, cycling or simply munching a picnic while enjoying a splendid view of the city. Walking and cycling trails pass small beaches and the remnants of abandoned military installations before reaching the island's 781ft (238m) summit. Between 1910 and 1940, some of the former military buildings were used to hold would-be immigrants (97% of them from China) before they were permitted, or denied as the case may be, entry to the USA. Most of the Chinese were intending to join relatives in San Francisco's Chinatown and some of their writings, often describing the harsh conditions they endured, have been preserved on the walls.

Below: *Sausalito is a popular launch site for windsurfing in the bay.*

Above: *Looking towards San Francisco from the Marin Headlands.*

Marin Headlands **

Commencing on the far side of the Golden Gate Bridge, the wild hills of the Marin Headlands provide a vivid backdrop for San Francisco and can be explored on a network of roads and many miles of walking trails.

The **Marin Headlands Visitors Center** is a useful source for the latest trail information and is within easy reach of the dark-sand **Rodeo Beach**, popular with surfers. A noted spot for enjoying a moonlit high tide, the beach divides the ocean from **Rodeo Lagoon**, whose still waters provide food for an abundance of birdlife.

On summer weekends, visits can be made to the **Point Bonita Lighthouse**, completed in 1855 and among the oldest fixed beacons on the US's west coast. Occupying a wind-tormented spot overlooking the entrance to the Golden Gate, the lighthouse lies at the end of a half-mile trail that navigates a tunnel hewn out of rock by hand in 1877, and a wooden bridge before reaching its conclusion.

A number of former military sites of major strategic importance dot the southerly reaches of the headlands. The earliest defences appeared here in the late-19th century, and during World War II installations for huge naval guns were put in place. The guns never arrived but the immense bunkers intended to hold them remain.

A Longer Trip: Fort Ross State Historic Park

An intriguing footnote in California's history lies 75 miles (120km) north of San Francisco on Highway 1, only accessible by car. Along this isolated and sometimes moodily fog-shrouded section of coast stand the restored buildings of Fort Ross State Historic Park (daily 10:00-16:30), built in the traditional style of their homeland by a group of 95 Russians who arrived in 1812. Exhibits in each building describe the workings of the settlement, established to hunt, trade with natives, and grow food for Russian fur-trappers in Alaska. Be prepared for a loud bang at 15:00, when the Russian cannon is fired and its blast reverberates for miles.

Audubon Canyon Ranch

For many visitors to San Francisco, the rich proliferation of bird life provides reason enough for venturing north over the Golden Gate Bridge. On weekends between mid-March and mid-July, devoted twitchers should take the side road just north of Stinson Beach that leads into Audubon Canyon Ranch, a 1000-acre (405ha) bird refuge and research centre with footpaths bringing splendid views of egrets and great blue herons during their nesting period. For the ornithologically uninitiated, a small museum documents the intricacies of local bird life.

Stinson Beach and Bolinas Lagoon **

Being sheltered from northerly winds by the Bolinas Peninsula, the 3-mile long (5km) **Stinson Beach** enjoys sunny and warm conditions even when much of the coast is shivering. Many San Franciscans come here to sunbath, surf and swim (only permitted between mid-May and September, when lifeguards are on duty). Immediately north, the shallow waters of the **Bolinas Lagoon** attract thousands of egrets and herons, while the lagoon's many sandbars make perfect resting spots for seals. Nearby is the **Audubon Canyon Ranch**, a nature reserve and research centre that opens to the public between mid-March and July.

Muir Woods National Monument and Mount Tamalpais **

Able to reach 350ft (107m) in height, the slender redwood is the world's tallest tree and is found only in groves along a narrow stretch of the northern California and Oregon coast where the damp, misty conditions prove ideal. The redwood grove of Muir Woods National Monument, on the appropriately named **Panoramic Highway**, 12 miles (19km) north of the Golden Gate Bridge, may not hold the tallest examples but does give a good impression of the awesome stature of these mighty trees. The grove lies at the end of a short walking trail from the car park. From the monument's car park, the Panoramic Highway continues deep into Mount Tamalpais State Park, an area covering approximately 6200 acres (2511ha), which serves as a giant playground for Marin County, and then on to **Mount Tamalpais** itself. From the 2571ft (784m) summit there are unforgettable views across the Bay Area and far beyond.

Below: *The breathtaking view from the summit of Mount Tamalpais, 2571ft (784 m) high.*

San Francisco at a Glance

Best Times to Visit

Though fogs are common in the early morning and evening, San Francisco enjoys a mild year-round climate and can be visited at any time. The fogs are generally at their worst during the summer, leaving September and October as the sunniest and most pleasant months. Temperatures seldom drop to uncomfortable depths during winter, although January brings San Francisco's heaviest rainfall.

Getting There

Arrival by Air
San Francisco International Airport, tel: (650) 876–7807, is approximately 14 miles (22.5km) south of the city. Privately run **minibuses**, such as Airport Express (tel: (415) 775-5112) and Super Shuttle (tel: (800) 258–3826) will collect arriving passengers from the traffic island directly outside the terminal and transport them to most central points in San Francisco for around $5 a person.
Alternatively, the SFO Airporter (tel: (650) 624–0500) is a large **coach** operating every 20 minutes (05:00–23:00) between the airport and hotels around Union Square. The one-way fare is slightly less than that of the minibuses, and buying a round-trip ticket brings a 50% overall reduction.

Considerably less costly are the KX and 292 **buses** operated by the local SamTrans bus service (tel: 800/660 4BUS). The KX is an express service, making only a few stops on the 35-minute journey from the airport to San Francisco's Transbay Terminal (at First and Mission streets). The 292 makes more stops and takes 20 minutes longer to complete the same journey. Exact change is required on both buses and luggage on the KX is restricted to one moderately sized item. SamTrans buses call at marked stops outside the airport's United and Delta terminals. **Taxis** are plentiful at the airport, and taking one into the city will cost $30–40 and take 30–50 minutes depending on traffic.

Arrival by Land
Northern California's freeways and highways provide direct **road access** to the city via the Golden Gate or Bay bridges (toll payable on each). San Francisco is a two-hour drive from Sacramento or Santa Cruz, and 8 hours from Los Angeles.
Direct **Greyhound buses** are frequent from Los Angeles and Sacramento; much less so from other parts of California. **Amtrak trains** stop on the east side of the bay at Emeryville, from where **free coaches** carry passengers into the city.

Getting Around

A compact city filling the tip of a peninsula, San Francisco is quick and simple to travel around and a car is not essential. Many adjoining neighbourhoods can be easily and safely explored **on foot** and, where distances are greater, a comprehensive **bus network** is inexpensive and simple to use.
The **BART** (Bay Area Rapid Transit) underground train system is a highly efficient alternative to buses across larger distances, notably to Berkeley and Oakland; **ferries** link the city with Marin County and Oakland.

Buses and streetcars
Passenger services on San Francisco's streets include buses and electrically powered streetcars operated by **MUNI** (Municipal Railway) (tel: (415) 673–MUNI).
All MUNI routes are shown in the phone book and at most bus stops. All journeys require a flat fare (no change given) to be paid into the machine next to the driver on boarding. Free transfers (valid for two hours) onto other routes are issued by the driver on request. Most MUNI services run from 05:00–01:00, with a greatly reduced **'Owl Service'** serving the main routes through the early morning hours. Convenient and economical is the **MUNI Passport**, a one-, three- or

San Francisco at a Glance

seven-day ticket allowing unlimited travel on buses, streetcars and cable cars, and obtainable from City Hall and from shops displaying the MUNI sign.

Cable cars
Though a familiar emblem of the city, cable cars provide a very limited service and operate on just **three routes**: two between Market Street and Fisherman's Wharf, and one between the Financial District and Nob Hill. Nonetheless, cable cars are enjoyable and tickets can be bought from self-service machines at end points of the routes before boarding a car.

BART
The BART system is useful for journeys from San Francisco under the bay to Berkeley and Oakland and also for swift links between the Financial District, Civic Center and the Mission District. Tickets are priced according to distance travelled and can be bought from self-service machines at BART stations. The system runs from 06:00–00:00 (08:00–00:00 on Sundays). For information, tel: (415) 992-BART.

Ferries
Angel Island, Oakland, Sausalito and Tiburon, and other points on and around San Francisco Bay can all be reached by ferry. Departures are from the **Ferry Building** and from **piers 39, 41 and 43** at Fisherman's Wharf. The major operators are Golden Gate Ferries (tel: (415) 923–2000); Red and White Fleet (tel: (1–800) 229–2784) and Blue and Gold Fleet (tel: (415) 705–5555). These companies' scheduled ferry crossings are considerably cheaper than taking a sight-seeing cruise (see below) and offer excellent views of the city and its bridges.

Taxis
Taxis can usually be found around major transport termini and outside major hotels, or hailed with relative ease on busy streets. It is also common to phone for a taxi (many are listed in the *Yellow Pages*). During rush hours, finding a taxi is likely to involve a lengthy wait; you will also be charged for sitting motionless in traffic.

Where to Stay

San Francisco offers quality accommodation in all price ranges, from **hostel beds** aimed at impecunious back-packers and plain and inexpensive **motel rooms** – invariably equipped with double bed, colour TV, telephone and bathroom – to **luxury hotels** where in-room jacuzzis and fax machines are taken for granted. In addition, there are a number of **bed and breakfast** inns, often atmospheric, converted Victorian homes with four-poster beds, claw-foot bathtubs, antiques in every corner, and a congenial host.

Advance booking is always advisable (by phone, fax or letter) to get precisely what you want – especially where bed and breakfast inns are concerned – though rarely, except during major holidays and conventions, will finding accommodation on arrival be difficult. The **San Francisco Convention and Visitor Bureau** publish the excellent *San Francisco Lodging Guide*, available free from their office on Hallidie Plaza (*see* p. 122), where you will also find countless leaflets on hostels, motels, hotels, and bed and breakfast inns; discounts are often offered on their standard rates simply by showing up (though phone first) with the leaflet.

Downtown San Francisco
Luxury
Campton Place Kempinski, 340 Stockton Street, tel: in California (1–800) 235–4300, elsewhere in USA (1–800) 426–3135, fax: (415) 955–5536. Top-class service from friendly staff make this medium-sized hotel a favourite of the discerning, well-heeled visitor.

San Francisco at a Glance

It may be a recent addition to Nob Hill's collection of luxury accommodations, but this artfully designed hotel within an historic building is not bettered by any of its neighbourhood rivals. If money is no object, opt for a room on the elite club level where the delights include all-day free snacks and drinks.

Mid-range

The Mansions,
2220 Sacramento Street,
tel: (1-800) 826 9398,
fax: (415) 567-9391.
An antique-filled bed-and-breakfast niche that comprises two adjoining 19th-century homes; the rooms vary in size and style.

Pacific Heights Inn,
1555 Union Street,
tel: (1-800) 523-1801,
fax: (415) 776-8176.
The affordable rates are a pleasant surprise, given the excellent location amid Pacific Heights' showpiece shops and restaurants, although the actual rooms are standard motel style.

Civic Center, SoMa, Mission District and the Castro

Luxury

The Palace,
2 New Montgomery Street,
tel: (1-800) 325-3535,
fax: (415) 543-0671.
Accommodating the rich and famous since before the 1906 earthquake and fire, this landmark hotel was purchased by Sheraton and given a $60-million face-lift before reopening in 1991. The result is luxury beyond belief.

Mid-range

24 Henry,
24 Henry Street,
tel: (415) 864-5686,
fax: (415) 864-0286.
This comfortable five-room guest house in a leafy Castro residential street makes an excellent base for gay travellers.

Budget

European Guest House,
761 Minna Street,
tel: (415) 861-6634,
fax: (415) 621-4428.
Pitched at backpackers with tidy four-bed dormitories and a friendly atmosphere in a useful SoMa location.

Pontiac Hotel,
509 Minna Street,
tel: (415) 863-7775,
fax: (415) 552-4491.
Ideally placed for seeing SoMa and using city-wide public transport, this extremely inexpensive hotel offers clean rooms without frills.

Haight-Ashbury and Golden Gate Park

Mid-range

The Red Victorian,
1665 Haight Street,
tel: (415) 864-1978,
fax: (415) 843-3293.
In the midst of Haight-Ashbury and in mood and decor perfectly mixing the spirit of 1960s San Francisco with 1990s new-age California; a wholefood breakfast is included.

Stanyan Park Hotel,
750 Stanyan Street,
tel: (415) 751-1000,
fax: (415) 668-5454.
Spacious Edwardian hotel, opposite Golden Gate Park and perfectly placed for exploring Haight-Ashbury; breakfast included.

Victorian Inn on the Park,
301 Lyon Street,
tel: (415) 931-1830,
fax: (415) 931-1830.
Overlooking the Panhandle, this rambling 1897 house is now a cosy bed-and-breakfast spot, attractively furnished with antiques and photos of old San Francisco.

Where to Eat

Ranging from low-cost, high-cholesterol breakfasts served in a street corner coffee shop to gourmand-pleasing morsels artfully served in the trendiest restaurant, San Francisco has food and eating places to suit all appetites and budgets. Long enjoying one of the largest concentrations of Italian and Asian restaurants in the US, San Francisco is noted for its eclectic tastes and has become synonymous

San Francisco at a Glance

with quality dining at very fair prices.

Downtown San Francisco
Luxury
Aqua, 252 California Street, tel: (415) 956-9662. The freshest seafood served in delicate, artful portions to a chic crowd in subdued surrounds.

Stars, 150 Redwood Street, tel: (415) 861-7827. A place to be seen for the city's socialites, particularly on their way to or from the opera. The food is generally top-notch American fare devised by one of the city's noted chefs.

Mid-range
John's Grill, 63 Ellis Street, tel: (415) 986-0069. The food is good quality all-American steak and seafood fare but the reason to pay a call is the Dashiell Hammett connection – the writer's fictional sleuth, Sam Spade, regularly dined here and is remembered by memorabilia in the upstairs dining room.

Miss Pearl's Jam House, 601 Eddy Street, tel: (415) 775-5267. Fiery Jamaican fare served to a fashionable crowd, accompanied by a reggae soundtrack and knock-out cocktails.

Budget
Dottie's True Blue Cafe, 522 Jones Street, tel: (415) 885-2767. A modern and health-conscious rendition of the traditional American coffee shop, with friendly service, low prices and many health-conscious options.

Indonesia Restaurant and Cafeteria, 678 Post Street, tel: (415) 474-4026. A justifiably busy place for a wide-ranging menu of finely prepared Indonesian dishes.

Yank Sing, 49 Stevenson Street, tel: (415) 541-4949. *Dim sum*, the Chinese lunchtime speciality of small dishes ordered from passing trolleys, is easily found in San Francisco. This outlet is slightly pricier than some but is among the best.

Chinatown, North Beach and Telegraph Hill
Luxury
Tommy Toy's, 655 Montgomery Street, tel: (415) 397-4888. For many years the city's most celebrated Chinese restaurant, creatively mixing ideas from Asian and French cuisine.

Mid-range
Brandy Ho's
450 Broadway, tel: (415) 362-6268. A local legend for delicious and spicy Hunan cuisine in an unpretentious setting.

Fog City Diner
1300 Battery Street, tel: (415) 982-2000. Upscale version of the classic American diner with traditional fare given a contemporary Californian twist.

Royal Jade, 675 Jackson Street, tel: (415) 392-2929. Features top quality Cantonese specials, wonderful *dim sum*, and also offers a lunchtime buffet.

The Stinking Rose, 325 Columbus Avenue, tel: (415) 781-7673. Serves a broad range of Italian dishes and seasons absolutely all of them with garlic.

Budget
Caffe Trieste, 601 Vallejo Street, tel: (415) 392-6739. There is no better place while touring North Beach for a pick-me-up coffee and a flavourful pastry than this North Beach landmark, in business since the 1950s.

House of Nanking, 919 Kearny Street, tel: (415) 421-1429. Northern regional Chinese cuisine served at prices low enough to make the wait – there is almost

San Francisco at a Glance

always a queue for a table – worthwhile.

Kowloon Vegetarian Restaurant, 909 Grant Avenue, tel: (415) 362-9888. Sports an immense menu of vegetarian versions of traditional Chinese fare, including a wonderful assortment of noodle dishes.

North Beach Pizza, 1499 Grant Avenue, tel: (415) 433-2444. Pizza devotees queue to get inside this long-running, late-opening eaterie celebrated for its substantial pizzas offered with a host of toppings. A second branch is close by at 1310 Grant Avenue.

The Northern Waterfront
Luxury
Greens, Building A, Fort Mason Center, tel: (415) 771-6222. Using produce grown on an organic farm, Green's serves expensive but ultra-healthy and caringly prepared vegetarian meals.

Mid-range
Gaylords, Ghirardelli Square, tel: (415) 771-8822. Excellent Northern Indian dishes served in a stylish setting with wonderful views through the oversized windows.

Budget
Eagle Café, Pier 39, Fisherman's Wharf, tel: (415) 433-3689. Order from the counter and wait for your number to be called in this 1920s diner, serving breakfast, lunch and dinner; a welcome find among the area's many tourist-aimed eateries.

Buena Vista Cafe, 2765 Hyde Street, tel: (415) 474-5044. The food is dependable and served in large portions but the real attraction is the splendid Irish coffee, a house speciality since 1952.

Cafe Marimba, 2317 Chestnut Street tel: (415) 776-1506 Lively and colourful spot for Mexican food, undergoing a resurgence of popularity in San Francisco; the dishes are primarily from the Oaxaca region.

Little Paris Coffee Shop, 444 Clement Street, tel: (415) 221-6028. The name suggests croissants and baguettes but the menu reflects the French influence in Vietnam, an enticing selection of Asian-Franco offerings for breakfast, lunch and dinner.

Nob Hill, Pacific Heights and Russian Hill
Mid-range
Elite Café, 2049 Filmore Street, tel: (415) 346 8668. The fiery Cajun and Creole of Louisiana treated to the subtleties of California Cuisine draws many discerning diners, and the creativity of the chef never seems to flag.

Perry's, 1944 Union Street, tel: (415) 922 9022. A long-established neighbourhood favourite serving no-nonsense meat and potatoes fare, be it thick burgers or juicy and tender steaks.

Budget
Doidge's Kitchen, 2217 Union Street, tel: (415) 921-9249. Breakfast regulars are well-heeled locals; the packed Sunday brunch is a Pacific Heights institution.

Civic Center, SoMa, Mission District and the Castro
Mid-range
South Park Café, 108 South Park Avenue tel: (415) 495-7275. A would-be French bistro opposite a little park on the edge of SoMa; starts the day by serving melt-in-the-mouth croissants and finishes it with a selection of cultured evening meals.

Budget
Ananda Fuara, 1298 Market Street, tel: (415) 621-1994. Variable but exclusively vegetarian fare, owned and operated by unobtrusive

San Francisco at a Glance

members of an Eastern religious sect.

Hamburger Mary's Organic Grill, 1582 Folsom Street, tel: (415) 626-5767. Neatly capturing the essence of offbeat SoMa, with vivid decor, vibrant music and a long menu of burgers, soups, sandwiches and much more.

Haight-Ashbury and Golden Gate Park

Mid-range

Thep Panom, 400 Waller Street, tel: (415) 431-2526 Hidden away on a side street, this excellent and affordable Thai restaurant is well worth seeking out for its long menu of delectably spiced and flavoured fare, and its friendly service.

Budget

Jammin' Java, 701 Cole Street, tel: (415) 668-5282. One of the neighbourhood's most mellow stops for coffee, cakes and healthy snacks.

Kan Zaman, 1793 Haight Street, tel: (415) 761-9656. Middle Eastern meals and snacks in an exotic setting aided by belly dancers and hookahs packed with Egyptian tobacco.

Richmond District, the Presidio, Lincoln Park and the coast

Mid-range

Hong Kong Flower Lounge, 5322 Geary Boulevard, tel: (415) 668-8998. High-class Cantonese restaurant serving great food in a splendidly ornate setting; the lunchtime *dim sum* is a treat.

Star of India, 3721 Geary Boulevard, tel: (415) 386-6208). At lunchtime, most diners opt for the money-saving buffet, but the menu carries a lengthy list of Indian fare, including many vegetarian dishes.

Straits Café, 3300 Geary Boulevard, tel: (415) 668 1783. Eclectic but uniformly excellent choice of fare, culled predominantly from the subtly spiced cuisines of Southeast Asia.

Budget

Mel's Drive-In, 3355 Geary Boulevard, tel: (415) 387-2252. Dispensing burgers, turkey sandwiches, milkshakes and many more all-American favourites to hungry customers since the 1950s.

CAFÉS

Found in every neighbourhood, cafés are an integral part of San Francisco life. They range from the long-standing Italian-American spots around North Beach, likely to have opera booming from the jukebox and scenes of the homeland decorating the walls, to the Bohemian hangouts of sections of the Mission District, where the clientele is typically a liberal intelligentsia perusing foreign-language magazines and indulging in lengthy chess matches. Most cafés serve light snacks, a few serve tea, but most are frequented for their coffee – a subject on which many San Franciscans claim to be connoisseurs – available in a multitude of styles.

BARS

Though it may seem San Franciscans would prefer to pass their idle hours in a café, the city has its share of bars, many of which are worth a visit for their history, their decor, their views – or simply for their beer. In the latter category are the San Francisco Brewing Company, 155 Columbus Avenue, Twenty Tank Brewery, 316 11th Street, and the Gordon Biersch Brewery, 2 Harrison Street, all of which brew their own beer to an impressive standard. For glorious views across the city, wait until sunset and sample the refined environs of the Top of the Mark, on the 19th floor of Nob Hill's Mark Hopkins Hotel, 1 Nob Hill, or the Carnelian Room, on the 52nd storey of the Bank of America building, 555 California Street.

San Francisco at a Glance

Closer to street level in every sense are The Saloon, 1232 Grant Avenue, which dates from 1861 and may well be the oldest bar in California, and Vesuvio, 255 Columbus Avenue, a favourite of the original Beats and of their modern-day admirers.
Many San Francisco drinking spots are decorated by interesting artworks but few can compare with the Sheraton Palace, 2 New Montgomery Street, where your pricey cocktail can be raised in toast to the wonderful Maxfield Parrish mural, said to be worth $2.5 million, behind the bar.

Tours and Excursions

Walking tours
Steep hills not withstanding, walking is the ideal way to see San Francisco and on-foot explorations are greatly improved with the **free walking tours** offered daily in different parts of the city by **City Guides**, tel: (415) 557-4266.
There are also numerous **paid walking tours**, among the best of which are **Wok Wiz**, tel: (415) 981-8989, covering Chinatown; **Cruisin' the Castro**, tel: (415) 550-8110) examining the city's gay and lesbian landmarks and lifestyles; and the **Flower Power Haight-Ashbury Walking Tour**, tel: (415) 836-1621, delving into Haight-Ashbury history with special reference to the halcyon days of the '60s.

Boat tours
Cruises on San Francisco Bay are offered by the **Red and White Fleet**, tel: (1-800) 229-2784) and the **Blue and Gold Fleet**, tel: (510) 705-5555.

Bus tours
If time is short, a sightseeing tour by bus is an ideal way to take in the major sights quickly; tours are offered by several companies, including **Gray Line**, toll-free tel: (1-800) 826-0202; and **Golden Gate Tours**, tel: (415) 788-5775.
A bus tour with a difference is **Three Babes and a Bus**, tel: (1-800) 414-0158, a four-hour Friday or Saturday evening jaunt to several of the city's leading nightclubs; tour price includes admission.

Shopping

From 25c chopsticks to thousand-dollar designer suits, San Francisco has something to tempt the most jaded shopper. Each neighbourhood has its share of unusual shops, and some sections of the city are noted for specialist retailing. Around **Union Square** are the city's most fashionable and dependable **department stores**, such as Sak's Fifth Avenue, 385 Post Street, Macy's, on either side of Stockton Street on the junction with O'Farrell Street, and Neiman-Marcus. Close by are some highly regarded local stores such as Gumps, 250 Post Street, purveyor of top quality china, porcelains and jewellery.
In moneyed Pacific Heights, **Union Street** holds high-fashion clothing stores and highbrow art and antique emporiums such as Artiques, number 2167, where absolutely everything for sale plays a tune. **Jackson Square** has become the base of the city's leading antique dealers, their wares filling rows of shopfronts with quality, expensive merchandise ranging from Persian rugs to finely crafted grandfather clocks from Europe. Whether in pursuit of 1920s evening wear or 1970s loon pants and platform boots, Haight-Ashbury's **Haight Street** is the place to seek out all manner of vintage clothing. More mainstream clothing is found in the many **factory discount outlets** of **SoMa**, often offering a 20%-40% savings on regular retail prices. One of the largest groupings of such stores is at Yerba Buena Square, 899 Howard Street.
Grant Avenue passes through Chinatown lined by kite shops, specialist tea traders, and browse-worthy general stores packed to the rafters with Oriental odds and ends. As Grant Avenue moves into **North Beach**, it becomes lined by more one-of-a-kind shops such as the studio store of avant-garde jewellery maker Peter Macchiarini, number 1529.

Travel Tips

Tourist Information

The **San Francisco Visitor Information Center**, Hallidie Plaza (weekdays 09:00-17:30, Sat 09:00-15:00, Sun 10:00-14:00), is packed with leaflets on sightseeing, accommodation, eating and much more, and multilingual staff are on hand to answer visitors' questions on all aspects of the city; tel: (415) 391-2000.

For information on the rest of California, contact the **California Office of Tourism**, 801 K Street, Suite 1600, Sacramento, CA 95814; tel: (916) 322-2881. In the USA, a toll-free number can be dialled to request a *Discover the Californias* brochure and state map; tel: (1-800) 862-2543.

Entry Requirements

All international visitors will need a full passport to enter the USA but may not need a visa if their intended stay in the USA is less than 90 days and they have a return ticket. A simple immigration form is issued prior to landing and this is collected at US passport control. Arrivals should be able to provide details of where they are intending to stay and show they have sufficient funds to last the duration of their visit.

Customs

Duty free allowances for arrivals aged 21 and over include a quart (1 litre) of alcoholic spirits or wine, 200 cigarettes or 50 cigars, and up to three gifts with a total value not exceeding US$100. Among items not permitted are meat, fruit, plants, chocolate liqueurs, and lottery tickets. Be aware that medications bought over the counter in other countries may be prescription-only in the USA.

Health Requirements

Provided travellers arrive from safe areas, no inoculations are required or recommended for entry into the USA.

Insurance

Insurance is not compulsory but is necessary to safeguard against potentially astronomical medical bills, as well as the usual recompense in respect of lost or stolen luggage and delayed travel.

Getting There

By Air: The national airlines of many countries have non-stop services to San Francisco. Some routings may necessitate a stop elsewhere in the USA before continuing to San Francisco, in which case arrivals must pass through customs and immigration at their first US stop. US-based travellers will find that most US domestic airlines have good links to San Francisco, although it may be cheaper to fly to Oakland and continue by public transport.

By Road: San Francisco is a long drive from anywhere in the USA or Canada and motorists will also have to cross deserts or mountain ranges on the way. Nonetheless, car enthusiasts who shun widely advertised and often economical fly-drive rental deals should take I-80, if approaching from inland, or Highway 101 if approaching from the north or south along the Pacific coast.

By Rail: Various discount fares periodically offered by Amtrak, the US rail passenger operator, can make travelling to San Francisco by train a relaxed and relatively inexpensive, if time-consuming, option. A daily service operates from Chicago to San Francisco, and another from Vancouver with stops in Washington, Oregon and San Francisco, before continuing to Los Angeles.

What to Pack

Pack clothing that can be worn in layers and peeled off as the temperature rises. Although generally mild, San Francisco's climate is rarely predictable and visitors should be prepared for cool, wet conditions even in the usually fine and dry summer, and for warm, sunny days in the otherwise cool and sometimes wet winter. Temperatures are also affected by morning and evening fogs that chill the warm summer days of July and August. Restaurant dress is tidy but casual with only the most formal dining places insisting on more elegant attire.

Money Matters

Banks: Mon-Fri 10:00-17:00 (or 17:30); some branches may open a few hours earlier or close a few hours later on selected days of the week. Some open Saturday 10:00–12:00.
Currency: US currency includes $100, $50, $20, $10, $5 and $1 notes of an identical size and colour, and variously sized coins: 25c (a 'quarter'), 10c (a 'dime'), 5c (a 'nickel') and 1c (a 'penny').
Currency exchange: Other than small amounts of cash, the easiest and safest way to carry money is as US-dollar travellers cheques, which can be used like cash in hotels, restaurants and certain shops. Most hotel cashiers will exchange US travellers cheques for cash, while it is more unusual for banks to do so – those that offer the service will usually request ID and may charge a commission fee. While acquiring US travellers cheques and currency before leaving home will save time and money, it is possible to exchange foreign currency and travellers cheques in San Francisco at banks with foreign exchange desks and at the city's exchange bureaux. These include: **American Foreign Exchange**, with branches at 315 Sutter Street, tel: (415) 391-9913; 124 Geary Street, tel: (415) 391-1306; and Pier 41, Fisherman's Wharf, tel: (415) 249-4667; **American Express**, 333 Jefferson Street, tel:(415) 775-0240; and 455 Market Street, tel: (415) 536-2600; and **Bank of America**, 345 Montgomery Street, tel: (415) 622-2541. There are also several foreign exchange desks at San Francisco Airport.
Credit cards: All major credit cards are widely accepted and commonly used; most motels and hotels will take a credit card imprint on arrival and deduct charges from this unless the guest requests otherwise. Without a credit card, payment for the first night, at least, must be made when securing a reservation or at check-in.
Tipping: Provided service is satisfactory, tipping is widespread and expected. In a restaurant or taxi tip 15%-20% of the bill; for a helpful hotel porter give $1 per bag.
Sales tax: Added to the marked price of everything you purchase is 8.5% sales tax.
Hotel tax: All San Francisco hotels are required to add the city's 12% transient occupancy tax to their room rates – which are usually advertised or quoted without this tax.

Transport

Car hire: The only practical way to travel much beyond San Francisco, other than by air, is by car. All major car rental firms have offices throughout the city and at the airport. For citizens of most countries a full driving licence is all that is required to rent a car; charges rise for drivers under 25, and only **Budget** rents to drivers under 21. Unless requested otherwise, all rental cars will have automatic transmission. Payment should be made by credit card, or otherwise a sizeable deposit will be required in cash or travellers cheques. International travellers may find there are savings to be made by booking a car prior to arrival, or as part of a fly-drive package. Within the USA, major car rental companies can be reached on toll-free numbers.
Avis, tel: (1-800) 331-1212; **Budget**, tel: (1-800) 527-0700; **Dollar**, tel: (1-800) 800-4000; **Hertz**, tel: (1-800) 654-3131; **National**, tel: (1-800) 227-7368; **Thrifty**, tel: (1-800) 367-2727.

Road rules and signs:
On interstates (the main fast-

moving, multi-lane routes that crisscross the entire country) there is usually a marked speed limit of 55mph (89kph) or 65mph (105kph) in California and some sections may have signposted minimum speeds. Generally smaller and slower are the state highways and a few county roads. Although speed limits are commonly exceeded, on-the-spot fines can be imposed for doing so. Lower speed limits are signposted in towns and cities. Driving with an open alcohol container in the car is an offence, regardless of whether or not the driver has been drinking; any measurable alcohol in a driver's blood constitutes drunk driving and is a serious offence.

Petrol: Compared to most countries, petrol is extremely cheap and petrol stations are plentiful in all but the most remote areas.

Safety when driving:
When driving, plan your route carefully. In cities use freeways whenever possible. Do not stop to assist an apparently broken-down vehicle but report the incident to the **state highway patrol** from the next phone. Similarly, if your car breaks down in a remote area, stay inside with the doors locked until a passing highway patrol car comes to your aid.
Rental cars will also have a number prominently displayed to call if the car breaks down in a busy locality.

Air: Numerous regional airlines operate in and around California and many advertise off-peak discounted fares. These usually involve travelling on stand-by (without a confirmed reservation but able to board when a seat becomes available), which may be inconvenient but can save money. Also worth looking out for are flight and hotel packages to nearby resorts such as Lake Tahoe and Palm Springs in California, and Reno and Las Vegas in Nevada.

Trains: Anti-pollution initiatives have led to increased passenger services on California's few rail passenger routes, though many towns are several hours by road from the nearest station and passengers are conveyed to the trains by bus. As yet, however, rail travel is more of a novelty than a practical means of getting about. Scenic routes include the **Coastal Starlight** between Los Angeles and San Francisco. All US rail passenger services are run by **Amtrak**, tel: (1-800) USA RAIL.

Buses: Greyhound buses (tel: toll-free 1-800 231-2222) provide services throughout California and across the USA, but within the state are only frequent and reliable between San Francisco, Sacramento, Los Angeles and San Diego.

Business Hours

The San Francisco business day generally begins at 08:00 or 09:00 and ends at 16:00 or 17:00. Usual banking hours are Mon-Fri 10:00-17:00 or 17:30, although some branches may open or close a few hours earlier or later on selected days of the week. Typical shop hours are weekdays and Sat 09:00 or 10:00 to 17:00 or 18:00. Department stores and shops in popular tourist areas are likely to keep longer hours and may be open on Sundays too.

Time Difference

San Franciscans set their clocks to **Pacific Standard Time**, which is 3 hours behind the US East Coast, 8 hours behind the UK, 9 hours behind the rest of Western Europe, and 16-18 hours behind Australia. The time difference may vary by an hour during the **Daylight Saving** time period, in effect from the first Sunday in April to the last Sunday in October.

Conversion Chart

From	To	Multiply By
Millimetres	Inches	0.0394
Metres	Yards	1.0936
Metres	Feet	3.281
Kilometres	Miles	0.6214
Kilometres square	Square miles	0.386
Hectares	Acres	2.471
Litres	Pints	1.760
Kilograms	Pounds	2.205
Tonnes	Tons	0.984

To convert Celsius to Fahrenheit: x 9 ÷ 5 + 32

Communications

Post: Postal services into and out of San Francisco are generally swift and reliable; mail sent to US addresses must include the letters and numbers that form the zip code. Stamps are available from post offices and (more expensive) vending machines in hotels. Post offices are generally open Mon-Fri 08:00-18:00 and Sat 08:00-13:00. Post office locations are given in the phone book.

Telephones: Public telephones are easy to locate in San Francisco and most local calls cost from 30c; insert coins before dialling (no change given). Calls from hotel room phones are liable to be much more expensive than calls on public phones, though some hotels offer free local calls from rooms. Many businesses can be called on toll-free numbers (prefixed 1-800, 1-888,1-866), which do not require any coins to be inserted. Some hotels, however, charge for toll-free calls made from rooms. Businesses may also make use of US telephones' letter and number dial to express their telephone number as easily remembered words, for example Amtrak's toll-free tel: (1-800) USA-RAIL.

Email and Fax: Widely-found cybercafés and some public libraries offer internet access for email. Most accommodations have fax machines and will send a fax on guests' behalf though many charge (and some charge steeply) for this. Some hotels also charge for receiving faxes on guests' behalf.

Electricity

The US electrical supply is 110 volts (60 cycles) and appliances use two-prong plugs. Appliances designed for other voltages can only be used with an adapter. Many electrical goods, such as computers, VCRs and CD players, are less expensive in the USA but may be unusable in other countries; check before buying.

Weights and Measures

The USA uses the Imperial system of weights and measures, though the US gallon and pint are each roughly 80% of their Imperial counterparts.

Health Services

As with the rest of the USA, high standards and high costs are the main traits of San Francisco's health services and visitors are strongly advised to be **adequately insured** for even minor medical treatment. Hospitals with a 24-hour casualty department include **San Francisco General**, 1001 Potrero Avenue, tel: (415) 206 8000; and the **Medical Center** at the University of California, San Francisco, Parnassas Avenue at Third Avenue, tel: (415) 476-1000. To call an **ambulance** in an emergency situation, use the free emergency number, tel: **911**. For non-emergency need of a doctor or dentist, look under '**Physicians and Surgeons**' or '**Dentists**' in the Yellow Pages, but calling out a doctor or dentist can be very expensive, even before they provide any treatment. **Pharmacies** are plentiful but many drugs available elsewhere require a prescription in the USA and may have different names. If intending to buy prescription drugs, bring a note from your own doctor. San Francisco has several late-night pharmacies and there are two 24-hour branches of **Walgreen:** 3201 Divisadero Street, tel: (415) 931 6417); and 498 Castro Street; tel: (415) 861 6276.

Public Holidays

1 January • New Year's Day
3rd Monday in January • Martin Luther King's Birthday
12 February • Lincoln's Birthday
3rd Monday in February • Washington's Birthday
31 March • Cesar Chavez Day
25 May • Memorial Day
4 July • Independence Day
1st Monday in September • Labor Day
2nd Monday in October • Columbus Day
11 November • Veteran's Day
4th Thursday in November • Thanksgiving Day
25 December • Christmas Day
Good Friday is a half-day holiday.

Personal Safety

San Francisco is a generally safe and enjoyable city though visitors should heed common sense precautions. These include not carrying easily snatched bags and cameras, not carrying a wallet in your back pocket, and whenever possible leaving valuables stashed in your hotel's safe. Report any stolen items to the nearest police station, the address of which will be in the phone book. Avoid poorly lit areas, that may seem deserted, or obviously run-down areas. Most San Francisco neighbourhoods are relatively safe, although parts of the Mission District, the Western Addition (east of Haight-Ashbury) and the Tenderloin (east of Civic Center) have their share of contemporary urban problems and can be dangerous as a result. Wherever you are in the city, if somebody speaks to you on the street they might not be harbouring hostile intentions but should always be treated with some suspicion.

Emergencies

Fire, police or ambulance, tel: **911**. No money required. The city also has emergency numbers and help lines for specific troubles or crises, all listed in the local phone book.

Holidays and Festivals

Banks and all public offices are closed on public holidays, although shops may be open on some. Whether staged to celebrate ethnic heritage, sexual preferences, love of music or simply to provide an excuse to dress up, the city has **festivals** galore almost all-year round.
During the **Chinese New Year** (late February or early March, depending on the lunar cycle), dragon costumes and firecrackers are commonplace in Chinatown; the event culminates in a large and noisy parade along Grant Avenue. **St Patrick's Day**, on the Sunday nearest to 17 March, sees Irish-themed events throughout the city and a parade along Market Street. In April, the ethnic spotlight shifts to the Japanese with cultural events in Japantown to mark the **Cherry Blossom Festival**.
The Mexican celebration of **Cinco de Mayo** (5 May) brings two days of festive happenings to the Mission District. **Lesbian and Gay Freedom Day** in June is among San Francisco's biggest and brashest festivals with gays, lesbians and their friends parading from the Castro to Market Street.
San Francisco's climax to **Independence Day**, or 4 July, is a firework display at Crissy Field on the Northern Waterfront.
By contrast, August's **cable-car bell ringing contest** in Union Square is unique to San Francisco, as is the same month's **Bay-to-Breakers Race**, in which thousands of bizarrely attired would-be athletes tackle the 7½ mile (12km) course from the bay to the ocean. September's **Jazz and Blues Festival** has internationally renowned musicians performing in the open air at Fort Mason Center. Besides its well-known trick-or-treat traditions, **Halloween** (31 October) has special relevance for San Francisco's gay population and is marked by a wildly costumed parade along Castro Street.
November's **Day of the Dead**, a Latin American festival to honour the spirits of the dead, brings macabre imagery and costumes to the Mission District. The final major festival of the year is **Thanksgiving**, a quiet family occasion centred around a turkey dinner eaten to commemorate the first successful harvest of the Pilgrim Fathers, who landed in New England in 1620.

Good Reading

- Bronson, William (1986) *The Earth Shook, the Sky Burned*. (Chronicle).
- Caen, Herb (1949) *Baghdad By The Bay*. (Comstock Editions).
- Dunlop, Carol (1982) *California People*. (Peregrine Smith).
- Genthe, Arnold and Tchen, John Kuo Wei (1984) *Genthe's Photographs of San Francisco's Old Chinatown*. (Dover).
- Gordon, Mark (1988) *Once Upon A City*. (Don't Call It Frisco).
- Iacopi, Robert (1978) *Earthquake Country: How and Why Earthquakes Happen in California*. (Sunset).
- Maupin, Armistead (1978) *Tales from the City*. (Chronicle).
- Mowry, Jess (1992) *Way Past Cool*. (Chatto & Windus).
- Seth, Vikram (1986) *The Golden Gate*. (Faber & Faber).
- Shilts, Randy (1993) *The Mayor of Castro Street*. (Penguin).
- Tan, Amy (1989) *The Joy Luck Club*. (Minerva).
- Woodbridge, Sally B, Woodbridge, John M and Byrne, Chuck (1992) *San Francisco Architecture*. (Chronicle).

INDEX

Note: Numbers in **bold** indicate photographs